T0306064

Project Management
Lessons Learned

Project Management Lessons Learned
A Continuous Process Improvement Framework

Mel Bost

CRC Press
Taylor & Francis Group
Boca Raton London New York

CRC Press is an imprint of the
Taylor & Francis Group, an **informa** business
AN AUERBACH BOOK

CRC Press
Taylor & Francis Group
6000 Broken Sound Parkway NW, Suite 300
Boca Raton, FL 33487-2742

First issued in paperback 2021

ISBN-13: 978-1-4987-4777-6 (hbk)
ISBN-13: 978-1-03-209527-1 (pbk)

Library of Congress Cataloging-in-Publication Data

Names: Bost, Mel, author.
Title: Project management lessons learned : a continuous process
improvement framework / Mel Bost.
Description: Boca Raton, FL : CRC Press, [2018] | Includes bibliographical
references and index.
Identifiers: LCCN 2018006945 | ISBN 9781498747776 (hb : alk. paper) |
ISBN 9780429490361 (e)
Subjects: LCSH: Project management. | Leadership. | Organizational
behavior.
Classification: LCC HD69.P75 .B67 2018 | DDC 658.4/04--dc23
LC record available at https://lccn.loc.gov/2018006945

Visit the Taylor & Francis Web site at
http://www.taylorandfrancis.com

and the CRC Press Web site at
http://www.crcpress.com

This book is dedicated to my wife Linda Bost, my daughter Christina H. Bost Seaton, my son-in-law Mike Seaton, and my granddaughter Quinn Penelope Seaton.

Without their encouragement, this dream would not have become a reality.

Contents

List of Figures

List of Tables

Preface

Why is "Success" magazine so successful?

Is it because the articles are so skillfully written that the readers feel compelled to read the magazine cover to cover?

Is it because the insights are so insightful that no reader can resist the articles?

Is it because John C. Maxwell always seems to grace their pages with his deep insights into leadership?

No.

It's because everybody, no matter what their chosen field or discipline or career path, wants to improve their performance and happiness in their chosen field. People are searching every day for that bit of wisdom that will give them a clue about their own lives and their own happiness.

And you, as a reader of this book, are not an exception.

It's why you have picked up this book. If you are a seasoned project manager or just an aspiring young project manager or a practitioner from another discipline or field, the idea that something learned may contribute to your achievement and happiness is important. Besides, project Lessons Learned is even more important because everyone takes on projects large and small, formal and informal, approved and unapproved, budgeted and unbudgeted, each day.

This book is designed for anyone who desires to know more about project Lessons Learned, why they are important, and how to capture, document, and share them with others.

This book has three main sections.

The first section deals with PMO as a setting for projects, the project environment, project behavior, performance, and structure. This overview is intended to provide the reader with an understanding of how environment and policy can influence the overall behavior and performance of a group such as PMO.

The second section deals with project Lessons Learned from single projects. Every project manager has been faced at one time or another with capturing, documenting, and sharing Lessons Learned from projects. Besides being a Project Management Body of Knowledge Best Practice, it is also an activity recognized by most larger-project management organizations and communities in modern project work.

The third section deals with project Lessons Learned from multiple projects subject to the same project environment.

The focus of most project Lessons Learned activities is on the single project itself. What did the project team learn about its project behavior and actions that could be captured to benefit future project managers in the project community? However, very little work has been done on the other major contributing factor in project Lessons Learned. That is of course, the project environment. Every project is subject to (1) a project environment created by the organization and (2) the external environment in which people function every day. The neglect of the project environment as a major factor in capturing and documenting project Lessons Learned means that the focus on continuous improvement in the project community has been almost exclusively on the Lessons Learned from individual completed projects.

However, the potential for far-reaching leveraging actions to be taken regarding the project environment and the structure of that environment could benefit all future projects as well as provide meaningful insights into project team behavior. The resulting implications for knowledge management are just as great. Knowledge focused on the project environment can provide insights into how we design future project communities that are robust, productive, team inspiring, and can lead to greater success for all projects.

Every project manager takes on many roles in his or her career within their own or other similar project organizations and perhaps also in the larger project community. Every project manager should understand the concepts and application of the principles in the afore-mentioned part one. However, if a project manager is to succeed in a role such as "curator" (as defined by Charlene Li) for his own project organization or the wider project community, or if a project manager is to succeed in organizational effectiveness studies to improve his project environment, he needs to master parts two and three as well.

You will see that the emphasis throughout this book is on cap-turing, documenting, and sharing project Lessons Learned that are truly actionable for the organization. This is a formidable task. Even the most experienced project managers have difficulty applying this framework, because there are many considerations in choosing sig-nificant events from projects that are truly candidates for Lessons Learned and can be documented in a manner that supports continu-ous process improvement within the project context.

This book is intended to provide insights for project managers that can enrich their project management experiences and their careers. John C. Maxwell often says, "Why do people listen to and read books on personal improvement and development?" It is because they sin-cerely want to learn and grow and get better.

Please enjoy this text. My desire is that every project person who reads this book is energized to identify, capture, document, and share the project Lessons Learned that can truly add value and improve-ment to their project processes and to the stakeholders in general.

Now, let us learn about the importance of process to the discipline of project management.

Toward a Process State of Mind

I am sure that most of my readership are familiar with the Billy Joel song "New York State of Mind." Those of you around New York will recognize in this song some familiar landmarks and favorite places, which he says creates a "New York State of Mind." His longing for the old familiar of New York and its surroundings is particularly appeal-ing in this song, which has become one of my favorites.

I would like to use Billy Joel's theme to introduce my readers and friends to a concept I call "A Process State of Mind."

As I talk to friends and colleagues in the corporate world or who own their own small consulting firm, or who are engaged in activities in their communities every day, one thing they are all craving is "discipline" and "structure" and "organization" in their everyday lives and work.

They are all familiar with the concepts I have been writing about for the past few years in terms of PROCESS, PROJECT, and LESSONS LEARNED. And they have asked me for more descriptions of these practices in many cases.

Although I have offered my advice in individual cases as to how to obtain more "discipline," I thought it might be more meaningful to express it to all my readers in the form of a blog essay. So here goes!

While most of my writing and my book on Project Lessons Learned has focused on lessons learned and feedback to improve project management processes, these same concepts can be applied to any PROCESS. And PROCESS is, I believe, the very discipline that my readers and colleagues are seeking and need in their work and their lives.

A PROCESS is a "set of activities or tasks which, when performed in a prescribed sequence, yield a result or an outcome and which can be improved."

Yet, a process without some mechanism or format for improvement is not really a PROCESS.

As I talk to friends and colleagues, some basic questions come to mind that will make it easier for them to incorporate PROCESS into their everyday activities, so I would like to address some of these issues to bring us to a real "process state of mind."

First, who should be involved in making process improvements to a process? Ideally, the participants who plan and execute the process are best equipped to identify, document, and share "lessons learned" from the process, which can become "actionable" process improvements.

Second, if process improvements identified by the process participants seem to be few and far between, it may be that the process is coming close to optimization, although this state is hardly ever achieved due to the "dynamic" environment that most processes exist in.

Owners of the process should seek further improvements through Benchmarking or Best Practices.

The principles I have applied in this book on Project Lessons Learned can be applied to continuous process improvement scenarios, and I encourage my readers to look at the details as well as previous blog posts and essays about process.

But don't just take my word for it—here's another example of process improvement being employed in a discipline totally different from project management:

Doris Kearns Goodwin is considered by many to be "America's historian." She has written authoritative books about the Kennedys, Roosevelts, and Abraham Lincoln. But she will quickly tell you that the most asked questions in her lecture tours is about her childhood and the Brooklyn Dodgers.

She was born in Rockville Centre on Long Island, New York. Her father was a financial services employee who worked in Manhattan during the day. His desire to learn about the daily games of the Brooklyn Dodgers led him to teach Doris about the game of baseball using a small red scorebook to keep score. He taught her the shorthand symbols for scoring the game, such as "K" for strikeout and "1–3" in the scoring section for an inning (to indicate a put out by an infielder after a ball hit by the batter to the infield).

Each afternoon, Doris would listen to the radio broadcast of the Dodger games and record in her scorebook the events of the game. In the evening after dinner, she would sit with her father and recount the baseball game of the day.

"From something as simple as the small red scorebook in which I inscribed the narrative of a ball game, I saw the inception of what has become my life work as a historian," she says in her book *Wait Till Next Year*. "It would instill in me an early awareness of the power of narrative, which would introduce a lifetime of storytelling, fueled by the naive confidence that others would find me as entertaining as my father did."

Doris employed a PROCESS to achieve her objectives of bringing the daily baseball game summary to her father. She did not call it PROCESS then, but that is exactly what it was, a disciplined and organized way of achieving an objective each day.

And the little red scorebook we would term a PROCESS TOOL in today's process vocabulary. With the scorebook, she could answer her father's questions such as "How many strikeouts did Don Newcombe get today?" or "How many hits did Roy Campanella get today?"

In her process, Kearns Goodwin probably employed such questions as these to help her define the specific activities making up the process:

- What is game time?
- Is my radio tuned to the right channel?
- Do I need any other paper and pencil to make notes during the broadcast?
- Are there any terms Dodger announcer Red Barber has used recently that need clarification?
- Will my father and I review the game at the same time and location as usual?

This PROCESS served Doris Kearns Goodwin well in meeting her objectives. And I am sure that she identified process improvements along the way. At one point in her book, she recounts that at particularly tense moments in some games, she would actually mimic the voice and expressions of Red Barber to add realism and interest....a form of process improvement.

So let's create a "Process State of Mind" by looking for every opportunity in our organizations and in our lives to define processes that lead to meaningful outcomes and which can be improved. The structure and organization that will introduce to your daily activities will give you a good feeling for day-to-day living.

Note to the Reader:

In this book, the word "event(s)" has two connotations. For the case in which I am discussing single projects, an "event" is either a candidate for a lesson learned or an actual lesson learned. It is a significant occurrence or a scenario within a project. More than one "event" may be identified as a candidate or an actual lesson learned for a project. In fact, it is usually the case that 5–10 significant "events" are identified as project Lessons Learned for each project and then documented as shown in the text.

For multiple projects, the word "event(s)" refers to a single project within a defined project environment. Patterns of behavior may be observed and documented for several projects or "events" within that project space or environment.

How to Use This Book Successfully

Project Managers who follow and complete the case studies in this book will use the Project Lessons Learned Template to capture, document, and share Lessons Learned. The Template is as follows:

What was the expected result?	Examine project plans, assumptions, deliverables, risk management plans, business case, and financial case for the specific events.
What was the actual result?	Analyze actual performance versus expected performance for significant events. See chapter on selection of candidates for Lessons Learned.
What is the gap?	For each significant event, define the gap between expected and actual in as much detail as you can.
What is the Lesson to be Learned?	For each significant event: Summarize in detail the Lesson to be learned; Cite risk, new technology, prove-out, and key factors.
Comments	

Charlene Li, in her book *Open Leadership: How Social Technology Can Transform the Way You Lead*, identifies five levels of engagement by which project practitioners may interact with the project community:

Level One—Watching
Level Two—Sharing
Level Three—Commenting
Level Four—Producing
Level Five—Curating

If you aspire to be a "curator" of the project community, the insights you gain through observing and identifying patterns of behavior, systemic structures, mental models and vision will be invaluable to you as you mature in your aspirations. An aspiring "curator" should read and understand completely all three parts to this book.

For practitioners from other disciplines such as the legal industry, I encourage you to read this book so that you can begin to understand organizational dynamics in many organizational settings and not just your own chosen discipline. Particularly, be focused on the "Does

Structure Influence Behavior?" question. Wherever there are groups who organize themselves into specific units for the purpose of creating value through collaboration, discipline, and procedure, you will find these forces at work. But a new day may be dawning as I speak about in my Conclusions and Summary in which true learning organizations are on the horizon.

There are also exercises at the end of certain chapters to stimulate the thought processes of the reader.

Acknowledgments

I thank John Wyzalek for his support and encouragement in completing this book. I also thank Barry Cardoza for providing excellent suggestions to improve the manuscript. Also, I thank Rita Candolin-Gelber for her fantastic assistance in preparing the figures in this book.

I also thank my parents Ruth and Cletus Bost for instilling in me a love of reading at an early age and a desire to be a lifelong learner. They were always an inspiration.

I studied the process work of Peter Senge and John Sterman to understand organizational dynamics in terms of the reinforcing and balancing of feedback processes in organizations. Along with Daniel Kim's framework relating vision, mental models, systemic structure, patterns of behavior, and events, I began to understand how the performance of an organization can be affected by the behavior of its participants through the structure in place.

I want to thank Charlene Li for her "Rule of Engagement" for individuals when engaging a community. It led me to real insights about what the "curator" role means in a project community.

I want to thank Peter Guber, whose book *Tell to Win* emphasized to me the importance of storytelling in the bigger picture of communication and creating value with new initiatives and movements.

I want to thank Dr. Ziya Akcasu, Dr. James Duderstadt, and Dr. R. Joe Johnson for opening my eyes to the physical feedback processes that govern the way physical systems communicate in the natural and commercial world.

I also want to thank Wayne Thompson, author of the blog "Project Management War Stories" for encouraging me to share my PMO experiences from my blog through his podcasts on "PM War Stories." Our collaboration was excellent and insightful.

Finally, I want to thank my colleague Mark Price Perry of BOT International, whose leadership in his two books about PMO Setup and Project and Portfolio Management encouraged me to finish all my notes on this important subject Project Lessons Learned and the PMO environment.

Early in my career with Ford Motor Company, they enrolled me in a writing course at a local college. Although I felt that I was already a good writer, this course really opened my eyes to what a creative writer should focus on. Perhaps, the greatest lesson from this course, which I will never forget, was a single sentence: THE SECRET IS IN THE EDITING. How true this statement really is. Our original thoughts are all valuable and worth recording in a manuscript. But the real secret comes when we edit them into a work that others will want to read, that others will want to embrace, that others will want to emulate in their daily lives and work. THE SECRET IS IN THE EDITING.

Author

Mel Bost is a project management consultant specializing in project closeout and lessons learned, as well as process improvement, best practices, and benchmarking. For the past several years, he has been teaching "Project Management for Research" to postgraduate students at Arizona State University, as well as developing new approaches to the research process. He was formerly a practice leader in BOT International's Program Management Office (PMO) Practice, and he is a specialist in PMO best practices, project lessons learned, and program management. He is experienced in all aspects of project and program management, including strategic planning, design thinking, knowledge management, risk management, and business process analysis. Bost has successfully developed the processes, standards, procedures, and organizational structures for the PMOs of several major corporations. Before becoming a consultant, Bost worked for a number of large national and international companies, including Exterran Corporation, ConocoPhillips, Phillips Petroleum, Tosco Corporation, UNOCAL, Atlantic Richfield Company, and Ford Motor Company.

Bost began his career in industry with Ford Motor Company, where he directed product programs for the North American and European markets. He was also instrumental in a group that introduced finite element analysis in Ford Product Engineering using NASA programs.

With Atlantic Richfield Company, he directed Fuels Research and Development Projects. With UNOCAL and Tosco, he led Project and PMO programs. He was part of a global merger-transition team that developed business analysis and best practices for a new PMO before the merger of Conoco and Phillips Petroleum. He also led a global team to create a blueprint for implementing a PMO for Duke Energy Field Services and LUKOIL. Bost has worked with the PMO Executive Council in Washington, DC to define best practices for PMOs and with the Advisory Board of the University of Arkansas, Walton School of Business, Information Technology Research Institute. He is the author of the highly regarded blog, "MEL BOST PMO EXPERT," which addresses the structure, activities, and behavior of a PMO environment, and has also recorded numerous podcasts with Wayne Thompson of "Project Management War Stories."

In 2011, Bost was invited by the Panama Canal Authority to conduct two training courses in Panama with their Construction Division project managers, engineers, and other project personnel on the topic "Project Closeout and Lessons Learned." The Panama Canal Authority was engaged in a $5 billion program to expand the Canal, which was completed in 2015.

In 2012, in a cooperative effort between BOT International and Collaboration Management and Control Solutions headquartered in Dubai, Bost conducted a week-long training course in Dubai on Project Lessons Learned for several companies from Morocco, Saudi Arabia, and the United Arab Emirates. Collaboration Management and Control Solutions is one of the largest providers of project management training in the Middle East and Far East.

In 2012, in a joint effort by BOT International and ProjectManagement.com, Bost conducted one-day Project Lessons Learned training sessions in several U.S. cities. ProjectManagement.com is one of the largest online networks of project managers in the world.

Bost completed his BS in physics and MS in engineering degrees at Georgia Tech, and his MS engineering science and MBA degrees at the University of Michigan, Ann Arbor. He lives with his wife in the Scottsdale, Arizona area, and is an active volunteer with the University of Michigan Club of Phoenix.

1

INTRODUCTION TO PROCESSES AND PROJECTS AS KEY FACILITATORS OF MODERN LIFE

Life is the formation, development, and integration of "biological processes." Biological processes define us as human beings and are continuously changing as humans grow and develop. "Processes" facilitate their growth and development. All living organisms undergo major changes over time. Some of these changes may be considered "improvements" to the species, while other changes may be detrimental to the long-term viability of the species.

Individuals and organizations use "processes" and "projects" as key facilitators and tools of modern life. As we will discuss later, the ability of individuals and organizations to define and utilize processes and projects in their development is a maturity function. The same "basics" apply to both physical and biological processes. It is important to understand these basics before we tackle "lessons learned" in the context of "process improvement."

Individuals often go about their daily lives without really understanding how important Process is to their lives and livelihoods. This book is intended to provide insights into processes that the reader will grasp and use as they develop their roles in society.

Lessons Learned from process feedback actually forms the basis for human evolution and development. This book addresses an important aspect of lessons learned from the viewpoint that humans and organizations can take initiative and develop strategies from lessons learned to improve the Processes and Projects they use in daily life to accomplish their major objectives (Figure 1.1).

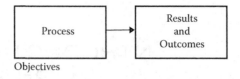

Figure 1.1 Process flow.

The Basics of Process

When you order a book from Amazon, mail a letter with the U.S. Postal Service, bake cookies at home, or withdraw some funds from your bank account, you are using Processes to help you accomplish some objective. Processes are facilitators and tools of modern life. By definition, a process is a set of "activities" or "tasks" which, when performed in a specific sequence, yields a *desired* result or outcome. The Activities and Tasks referred to in this definition can be complex and involve subprocesses themselves. Both individuals and organizations use processes to accomplish their objectives and functions.

The word "desired" in the definition of Process is significant because the first or even subsequent attempts to define and design a process that meets all objectives and achieves all results and outcomes is often unsuccessful. This introduces the need for Process Improvement. Understanding Process Improvement is key to the concepts of this book. It raises the questions "Where and how are process improvements identified?" and "Who is principally involved in process improvements?" (Figure 1.2).

The "Dynamics" of Processes

Time is a construct of man to give order to his environment. But Time introduces Dynamics into the concept of process. Because processes

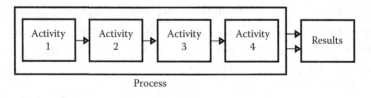

Figure 1.2 Definition of process.

require both human and physical resources to support their function and structure, roles and inputs to the activities may change over time. Dynamics therefore introduces the need for process improvement to maintain the desired outcomes of processes.

The "Sustainability" Implications of Process

Processes require "resources" for implementation and value creation. How efficiently these resources are used or how the processes utilize resources have sustainability implications. The initial design of processes, as well as process improvements, can consider Sustainability in design and function.

In his book *The Age of Sustainable Development*, Jeffrey Sachs argues that global strategies going forward must incorporate "sustainable development" goals, practices, and initiatives as the basis for approaching global development. How resources are utilized and dedicated to process definition and implementations going forward will be keys to our continued existence as a planet.

Processes as Major Components of Individual or Organizational "Capability"

Organizations and individuals develop "capabilities" that enable them to excel at the results and outcomes they achieve from focusing on their objectives. "Distinctive capabilities" are the things they excel at doing time and time again. Processes are a major component of Capabilities. Capability is the combination of people, processes, technologies, and organization that allows an individual or organization to deliver their intended outcomes.

For some highly technical industries such as software development or biopharmaceutical development, there are also "table-stakes" capabilities, which every company in that industry must develop as a baseline for competing in the industry (Figure 1.3).

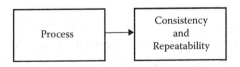

Figure 1.3   Measures of process maturity.

What Is Process Improvement?

Process improvements are introduced into the process discussion because

1. Initial and subsequent process design may not meet objectives, results, and outcomes.
2. Dynamics introduces the need for process improvements because of changes in resources, roles, and inputs over time.
3. Lessons Learned from the operations of processes create feedback that can improve processes. Lessons learned are usually identified by the people who are actively engaged in the process itself.
4. As new technologies replace old technologies, and new materials and resource types replace old, process improvement will be imperative. New process designs will be imperative for competitive and social needs.
5. Changes in regulatory requirements often drive process improvements.

When process owners introduce process improvements, they generally utilize industry and internally generated "best practices" or "benchmarking" to introduce changes into the Activities or Tasks that make up a process.

Capability Maturity and the "Well-Defined" Process

In 1979, Philip Crosby introduced a maturity grid/matrix applicable to organizations in his book *Quality Is Free*. It was known as the "Management Maturity Grid," and it described a progression of maturity in organizations related to management, moving from "ad hoc" activities and "quality," to a very mature state or environment in which Quality was embraced as the norm for all employees. Feedback was employed to improve activities and ensure quality.

In the 1980s, IBM's Watts Humphrey introduced a software development work based on the Management Maturity Grid. Over the past several decades, this work has been called "Capability Maturity Model" and has been extended from strictly software development to process development and process maturity for organizations generally.

The capability maturity model refers to the stages through which organizations evolve as they define, implement, measure, control, and improve their processes. The model provides a guide for selecting process improvement strategies. The highest state of maturity within the model is the "optimized" state in which "continuous process improvement" is the norm (Figure 1.4).

The discipline of software development also provided us with the concept of the Well-Defined process. A Well-Defined process is one which expresses and documents, for every major Activity and Task, the principal activities making up the task as well as any "entry" and "exit" criteria that add information to the Activity of Task in the form of what follow-up acts the Process Owner should expect other principal groups to take. Such topics as audit and quality control issues, regulatory issues, testing, and evaluation are often covered in Entry and Exit descriptions (Figure 1.5).

See Appendix 5 for more information about the Capability Maturity Model.

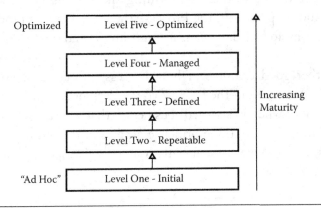

Figure 1.4 Capability maturity model.

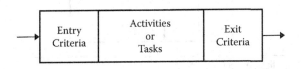

Figure 1.5 Well-defined process definition.

The Basic Principle of Process

Continuous process improvement begins with Process Improvement, which begins with "process." In order to talk about Process Improvement, we need a well-defined, working Process (Figure 1.6).

Familiar Impacts of Process on Business

In the movie *The Founder*, Ray Kroc (played by actor Michael Keaton) recognizes and acts on an innovative idea in fast food service and delivery, which was originally developed by the McDonald brothers in their San Bernardino, CA store. Tired and fed up with the poor service and food of the traditional drive in fast food restaurants in 1954, Kroc meets the McDonald brothers who used Process to revolutionize fast food preparation. In the movie, Kroc gets the brothers to focus on the actual Process of hamburger and French fry preparation. In one visual sequence in the movie, they discuss an ideal size for a restaurant and actually draw it with chalk on a tennis court. Then they proceed to define and redefine the food preparation process, taking into account the space allotted, the movement of workers performing the various tasks, and the inputs and outputs from the Process. The design of this process has implications for worker training, resources, and cost of the final product.

Another good example of how Process impacts business is the CNBC TV program "The Profit." Marcus Lemonis is an investor and entrepreneur who assists small businesses that are struggling financially. He focuses on three principle aspects of the business: People, Process, and Product. A particularly noticeable aspect of process is

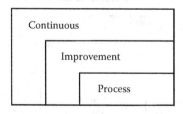

Figure 1.6   The basic principle of process.

that for multigenerational businesses, there is a high failure rate in the second or third generations because few processes are documented as it is difficult to repeat the experience and skills of the originator of the business.

Research as an Example of Process

Research is a good example of Process that most technical readers of this book will understand. In today's modern world, Research is the catalyst for innovation, entrepreneurial activity, personal expression of creativity, and growth for both individuals and organizations. It is integral to new product, service, and process development.

Research is a process that incorporates, in a specific sequence, Activities and Tasks, such as the development of a Hypothesis, the collection of Data, the assessment of the Data, the Empirical Testing of the Hypothesis based on the assessment of Data, and then the formation of a conclusion about the Hypothesis.

Research process improvement can include Benchmarking the various tasks and activities that define the process, or selecting Best Practices from other research efforts that may be applicable to the research process in question. In addition, the outcome and result of the Research Process can be assessed to determine if the objectives set out at the beginning of the research were met. Feedback from this assessment can be used to improve any activities and tasks of the Research Process.

Dynamics of the Research Process are often exhibited by the introduction of new methodologies for Data Collection and Assessment, which afford the researcher with new tools for assessing Hypotheses.

Capability Maturity of the Research Process can be addressed by examining the Research Process for a number of successive Research initiatives, to determine if the Process Owner exhibited "maturity" in the various Research initiatives he or she undertook. For example, if a Researcher has undertaken 20 Research initiatives, how many have been initiated in similar manner? Did the Researcher find a Best Practice among his research tasks and activities that he utilized in subsequent research initiatives? Does the researcher embrace improvement in a continuous fashion when undertaking new research initiatives?

Sustainability can also be applied to the Research Process if the process owner considers how Research Resources are utilized in his research.

See Appendix 6 more information.

The Basics of Projects

Projects are complex Processes usually used to convert "strategy" into "action" for both individuals and organizations. Projects usually require human and physical resources in their execution. They can result in bridges, buildings, new processes, or new products (Figure 1.7).

Projects are initiatives that generally have the following characteristics:

1. Specific start and finish dates
2. Dedicated human and physical resources
3. Defined scope and deliverables that are intended to produce an outcome
4. Defined activities and schedule to support the effort
5. Allocated or assigned budget related to scope of the project

As processes, projects can be improved in a number of ways. A comparison of expected and actual results from a project can yield "feedback" to improve the project process. This is the major subject of the book you are reading.

In the future, as more new technologies emerge from the drawing board, projects will contain more "technology development" in their planning and execution. New connotations for Best Practices and Benchmarking are sure to be recognized in this transition.

A good current-day example of new technology development and its impact on modern life is found in the work of Elon Musk, founder and CEO of TESLA. From electric battery development, space travel,

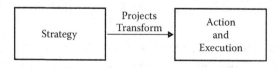

Figure 1.7   The rationale of projects.

ground transportation, and other ventures, he has demonstrated how technology will infuse new processes and projects in our lives.

Organizational Project Management Maturity Model

With the increasing focus by organizations that projects have a strategic role to create change in organizations and their operations, more emphasis is being placed on Organizational Project Maturity so that projects create repeatable and consistent results.

The methodology employed with Organizational Project Management Maturity Model (OPM3) is usually an assessment of the current maturity state of the project organizations such as Program Management Offices and then a process improvement program that focuses on increasing the organizational maturity (Figure 1.8).

The Basic Principle of Projects

All projects are processes but not all processes are projects (Figure 1.9).

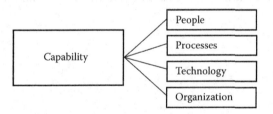

Figure 1.8 Elements in Organizational Project Management Capability.

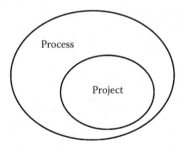

Figure 1.9 The basic principles of projects.

Conclusions

As a preliminary step in Lessons Learned in a project context and the feedback associated with the Lessons Learned that can be used to improve the project process, we have reviewed the foundation and some building block tools and facilitators for the discussion. This background and familiarity enhances our understanding of the context for Lessons Learned and process improvement.

In today's world, individuals and organizations set objectives for accomplishing many different initiatives relative to their lives and organizational viability. These initiatives can be complex and require human and physical resources to accomplish major tasks and activities relative to the final outcomes and results.

The quality of process improvement depends upon many factors, including the completeness with which the original process was defined and the dedication of the process owners to the principle that all processes can be improved.

Good process and project management practices are crucial in the modern world. Curators of process and project will seek to ensure that their colleagues and associates understand this crucial nature of both for future success.

2

UNDERSTANDING AND EMPOWERING THE PROGRAM MANAGEMENT OFFICE (PMO) AND ITS INFLUENCE ON PROJECT LESSONS LEARNED

I have been studying and writing about the structure, activity, behavior, development, and performance of Program Management Offices (PMOs) and project Lessons Learned for a number of years. I helped a major Fortune 500 company develop a robust project Lessons Learned process and framework for their PMO organization. I author a PMO blog known as *Mel Bost PMO Expert* and have contributed to several podcasts on the subject, which have been well received by the project community.

To those of you not so familiar with project Lessons Learned, let's start with a basic high-level project management process, that has four distinct phases, stages, or subprocesses.

Phase One—Initiation
Phase Two—Planning
Phase Three—Execution
Phase Four—Close

Project Lessons Learned are typically captured, documented, and shared at the conclusion of the major project activity so that they would naturally occur in the Phase Four Close subprocess. However, there is no rule that says that project Lessons Learned cannot be conducted at the end of each major phase, and we will discuss the advantages of doing this later in this book.

But, for beginners, assume that project Lessons Learned are captured, documented, and shared during the Project Close Process.

After talking with many PMO practitioners and project teams, I am seeing more companies currently looking for ways to close out their projects successfully. Many have turned to documenting and sharing project Lessons Learned as a close-out mechanism. Of course, this is a maturity issue. The more mature the organization is in its project management process, the more likely that organization is willing to invest the time and resources in closing out projects correctly with project Lessons Learned.

Many companies are looking for a framework for Lessons Learned. What I recommend to them is the standard framework: What was the expected outcome? What was the actual outcome? What is the gap? What is the lesson to be learned?

There is no doubt that those organizations who successfully convert project Lessons Learned to process improvement will gain a competitive advantage.

Another concept often used to characterize behavior and performance of an organization is maturity. Every organization exists at a particular maturity level depending on how it plans and executes the objectives defined within its organization.

Most characterizations of maturity use five levels of maturity:

Level One—Ad hoc or hero behavior
Level Two—Process defined for one project
Level Three—Consistent processes across all projects
Level Four—Metrics and benchmarking
Level Five—Continuous improvement

Organizations strive to increase the maturity level by adding discipline and framework, because, if they do, the results of their efforts are more repeatable and consistent. Lessons Learned is another one of those frameworks, which, if employed in a diligent manner, can improve the maturity level of an organization.

Some PMOs have been developed and nurtured by organizations in the past few years because of their success in converting strategy into action for organizations. Others have been formed because the organization believes it is the right thing to do in the face of stringent requirements like Sarbanes–Oxley. Originally conceived as part of an Information Technology (IT) Group to add discipline to the way IT projects were planned and executed, they have moved into Enterprise

PMO roles in many organizations and specialized roles in others. For example, Progress Energy has employed a Smart Grid PMO to lead its projects following the Smart Grid movement in electrical power generation and transmission.

Over the past few years, PMOs have evolved to incorporate more competencies such as vendor management and risk management in their portfolio of processes. In addition, they have developed skills and capabilities to handle complex project situations and juggle project portfolios in the face of constantly changing corporate and business environments. They have identified Best Practices and benchmarked their operations versus those of other PMOs.

They have also identified significant changes in resource types within PMOs as they have evolved and matured. Much as the Space Shuttle program saw its Shuttle Astronauts' skill requirements change from test pilots in the very early days to more payload specialist roles in recent times, PMO roles and resources have also shifted. In the early days of a PMO, Methodology and Best Practice experts abounded while some key resources focused on PMO processes. As PMOs evolved, the mix changed to more project managers who could successfully execute projects and portfolios of projects.

PMOs are reaching a point where increase in performance means "Just work harder."

But that is not the final answer.

Often, working harder without seeing an increase in performance can be a sign that there are barriers to improvement that need to be addressed. At present, I see a change coming in the focus of PMOs on performance enhancement. They are beginning to focus on organizational dynamics and organizational effectiveness. What that essentially means is returning to the old equation *actions and behaviors lead to outcomes or events* and examining all the variables that can impact actions and behaviors in the PMO.

Organizational dynamics is an area that has been studied in depth by researchers like Peter Senge, Daniel Kim, John Sterman, and William Braun for 20 or 30 years. What they have identified is a framework, which, on a level of reasoning basis, looks at vision, mental models, systemic structure, patterns of behavior, and events for an organization. The events are the actual observable actions in the organization. The equation *actions and behaviors lead to outcomes or events* is applicable. Researchers have identified a number of systemic structures called systems archetypes, which are recurring behavioral structural relationships in organizations. And since PMOs are a subset of the overall population of organizations, these systems archetypes apply to PMOs as well.

I first began to be aware of these organizational dynamics relationships when I worked for Ford Motor Company many years ago. Over the past 30 years or so, I have witnessed a number of these systems archetypes at work. They often bear simple names like "Limits to Growth," "Tragedy of the Commons," and "Growth and Underinvestment." We have all heard the age-old question "Does structure influence behavior?" meaning, "Do the policies, procedures, standards, and working relationships that are part of the organizational culture influence the behaviors and actions that the people take?" The answer is overwhelmingly yes.

I found this framework to be highly applicable to my work on project Lessons Learned in a project environment where several projects were subject to the same organizational or project environment. The key here is that understanding this behavior can lead to process improvements that leverage all projects when you look at modifying the project environment.

As PMOs evolve and become more mature in their influence in organizations, PMO practitioners must begin to recognize these systems archetypes at work and deal with the behaviors in the organization. Much of the remainder of this book addresses that subject.

3

WHAT DO I DO IF MY PMO CAN'T EXECUTE?

A number of years ago, the Los Angeles Dodgers and the Cincinnati Reds played a baseball game in which the Dodgers did nothing right and the Reds did nothing wrong. The final score was 10-0 in favor of the Reds. In a postgame press conference, the Dodgers Manager Tommy Lasorda was asked this question by a reporter, "How do you feel about your team's execution today?" Tommy thought a minute and then replied, "I am highly in favor of it."

Execution. Getting things done—consistent, coordinated, controlled execution. It's the road to success in today's competitive global marketplace. But how do you optimize that execution? How do you correct your Program Management Office (PMO)'s execution when you're not getting the expected results?

I would like to provide a perspective to this question based on my experience working in a PMO: observing the changes in its performance and identifying the actions that we undertook to optimize that performance.

As evidenced in the baseball game mentioned earlier, execution includes actions and behaviors, and decisions on the part of both teams lead to results. In a sense, we all develop or forecast expectations for those results before they occur, and then we measure the differences between the actual and the expected results.

That gap can be elusive because it contains not only team or group performance items but also individual performance items. It includes day-to-day decisions and judgments based on information we gather at or near the time of actions. It also brings the business context into play.

So optimizing the results from execution means understanding the gap between expectation and actual, and then providing feedback to change the execution. Sounds like there is a process lurking in there somewhere!

Let's look at an actual example. Some years ago, I was a member of a PMO following the merger of two major corporations. I had participated in the development of the processes, standards, and procedures for the PMO, so I understood the structure of the PMO quite well.

During the first year of actual operation following the merger, this PMO was mainly engaged in systems integration and applications/systems rationalization projects. As the two merged organizations combined their business systems, in most cases, they developed a single system where each had a different system before. An example would be the credit card networks of each company being merged into a single credit card system as a result of a PMO project.

The PMO delivered a number of projects during that first year so that, on a graph representing the number of projects completed versus the time to complete the projects, the upward trend was along a 45° angle. That performance defined the expectation for the PMO. Nobody stated that expectation as such, but everyone had the idea that the project teams were performing such that they could predict over time how many projects would be completed in the next incremental time frame.

After about one year in this mode, the emphasis shifted over to the PMO conducting projects for the business functional groups in the new merged organization. During the first year of the merged corporation, those groups had been forming and organizing, and not focused on systems projects addressing business needs. Over the next year of operation, the curve of projects completed versus time to completion began to flatten out and tended toward some asymptotic level. The PMO was no longer completing projects at a 45° clip.

What had happened?

Many of us formed a small group to study the structure and execution of the PMO at that point. We were aware that there had been a shift mainly from systems integration to new business functional group projects.

What we found was that there were two basic reasons why projects were lagging in execution.

First, the PMO had limited financial consulting resources for consulting with the business functional groups on their business-case economic analysis. Such financial consulting was a basic requirement for documentation of a complete business case and subsequent funding and approval of the project.

Second, we found that the PMO project coordinators and analysts were having difficulty translating the business functional area business requirements into project scope and business requirements for the projects. In other words, we were having difficulty framing the projects correctly to answer the question, "what problem am I trying to solve with this project?" Subsequently, there were a number of false starts and reframing of the projects, which led to fewer total projects completed over time versus those in the systems integration phase of work.

Now the first finding was easily addressed. The PMO added additional resources to assist with the financial analysis and in many cases partnered with Financial Services to coop those consulting resources.

Solving the second condition was a little more complex. When we examined it more closely, we found that the PMO project coordinators and analysts were not holding effective dialogues with the business functional groups to define the project business requirements. We immediately enlisted the help of Crucial Conversations training coordinators to teach effective dialogue within the PMO and business functional groups. Rapidly, we began to frame the projects correctly the first time, leading to effective and timely execution.

So, from a prescriptive point of view, what would I suggest you do if your PMO is not executing as expected?

First, look for alignment issues. Stephen Covey once said, "Every organization is perfectly aligned to get the results it gets." Alignment means that business processes, jobs, people, systems, rewards, and values and beliefs are aligned so that they support each other in the accomplishment of goals and objectives.

In the case in which business processes are changed, the other alignment variables must be addressed in order for results to be consistent with expectations. For example, if a business process is changed which involves a change in jobs and people, then systems and rewards as well as values and beliefs must also be addressed. Too often in the past, companies or smaller organizations within companies have changed business processes and the associated jobs and people without really addressing the systems, rewards, values, and beliefs that must support those process changes. A good place to learn more about this area is Michael Hammer's book, *Beyond Reengineering: How the Process*

Centered Organization Is Changing Our Work and Our Lives, as well as some of the publications by Booz & Company on organizational effectiveness.

Second, look for changes in objectives or goals or direction. In the example given earlier, the PMO shifted its emphasis from systems integration projects to business functional group projects, which meant that new sets of competencies might be necessary to continue with execution as it was expected.

Third, apply some systems thinking to the situation. Good resources on systems thinking are Peter Senge's *Fifth Discipline* and Daniel Kim's work. The high-level concept is described in the following paragraphs.

In systems thinking, the organization can be looked upon as a system that refers to organizational structure, culture, processes, procedures, feedback, human interactions, policies, and the structure we use to manage the process.

In systems thinking, we can see organizational processes as either reinforcing processes or as feedback processes. Reinforcing processes are those in which more is gained as we push harder on the variable defining the process. Balancing processes are those that tend to retard reinforcing processes.

As a general rule in systems thinking, if a growth scenario appears to be reaching a limits-to-growth situation, then look for the balancing loop that is tending to retard the growth of the reinforcing loop. Rather than continuing to push harder on the reinforcing loop, solutions can be more easily found in examining the balancing loop.

That is why solutions to the PMO scenario in which project completions were slowing were to be found in the balancing loop, which contained the financial/economic analysis as it contributed to the business case and the lack of effective dialogue promoting proper framing of the problem and poor business requirements definition.

Fourth, make sure that any major initiative or project that the PMO pursues has a robust organizational change management plan to ensure that all the stakeholders of the initiative or the project are addressed according to what is expected of them after the initiative or project is implemented. If you see results different from expectations following a major internal PMO initiative, look at the associated organizational change management plan to see how well it performed.

There may certainly be other perspectives on analyzing execution of the PMO and I invite others to comment on specific situations they have been involved in with PMO activity. We can all recall a myriad of interventions we have pursued within organizations to realign expectations and results. It is a never-ending job to continually examine alignment, but it is the only method for ensuring lasting, consistent Execution.

4

AVOIDING DISRUPTION OF THE PMO BY ACCIDENTAL ADVERSARIES

We had everything to gain by planning and working closely together to advance the development and maturity of our new IT Project Office, but it seemed that every time we would take a step together in the right direction, one of us would sideswipe the accomplishment by acting irrationally or in what seemed like an irrational manner.

Those were the words of my former manager in an Information Technology (IT) Project Office [a predecessor to the modern Program Management Office (PMO)]. It is an often-repeated statement, but one that does not get much scrutiny from a root-cause analysis format.

Here was the scenario:

A major energy company acquired the downstream assets of another energy company and integrated the functional groups, including the IT groups. At the start of this scenario, I was a project and planning consultant in the IT planning group. The IT group decided to form an IT Project Office, and it hired an experienced manager from a major Fortune 500 Company, whose expertise was in forming and maturing PMO-type organizations. Before that point, each IT Applications Development, Systems, and Infrastructure Group had planned and executed projects within their own groups with limited collaboration across groups.

A major consulting firm had facilitated the merger of the two energy companies, and management of the merged company strongly recommended that the IT group use the consulting firm as a guide in forming ITPO. The consulting firm had an excellent reputation for internal project management capability, and it utilized a methodology, which I will refer to here as the method. So, IT management was pleased at the outset that they not only had an experienced PMO-type manager, but also a strong consulting group direction.

The vision and directions given by the IT Project Office management to the consulting firm were that the ITPO wanted to instill its own trademark and business context in the new project group.

While the consulting firm heard this direction, it internally recognized that the firm had made a great investment in the method and that it would exploit the method at every opportunity.

The IT Project Office utilized the Software Engineering Institute's Capability Maturity Model as a framework for planning its path of evolution to a mature state. However, whenever a new process or procedure was developed in concert with the consulting group, the outcome had a strong flavor of the method. So, whenever the IT Project Office mapped its systems projects to follow the business processes with which it was trying to align, it conveniently left the consulting group out of the process until some redefinition of an omitted process was imminent.

This recurring pattern of behavior was subtle but highly visible to those of us living the daily ITPO experience.

This is an example of a systems archetype at work.

Peter Senge has written extensively about organizational dynamics and behavior and systems archetypes identifiable from events and patterns of behavior.

William Braun has also written extensively about systems archetypes. System archetypes are highly effective tools for gaining insight into patterns of behavior, themselves reflective of the underlying structure of the system being studied. The archetypes can be applied in two ways—diagnostically and prospectively.

Diagnostically, archetypes help managers recognize patterns of behavior that are already present in their organizations. They serve as the means for gaining insight into the underlying systems structures from which the archetypal behavior emerges. This is the most common use of the archetype.

Archetypes are effective tools for beginning to answer the question, "Why do we keep seeing the same problems recur over time?"

Prospectively, archetypes are useful for planning. See Appendix 2 for details. As managers formulate the means by which they expect to accomplish their organizational ends, the archetypes can be applied to test whether policies and structures under consideration may be altering the organizational structure in such manner as to produce the archetypal behavior. If managers find this to be the case, they can take remedial action before the changes are adopted and embedded in the organization's structure.

From my experience, archetypes can be highly effective when examining PMO and IT Project Office organizational structure (Figure 4.1).

The particular systems archetype described earlier is called accidental adversaries, because it explains how groups of people who ought to be in partnership with each other, and who want to be in partnership with each other (or at least state that they do), end up bitterly opposed. It applies to teams working across functions, to joint ventures between organizations, to union-management battles, to suppliers and manufacturers, to family disputes, and even to civil wars.

The classic case where this accidental adversaries structure was first articulated and recognized was a scenario involving Procter and Gamble (P&G) and Wal-Mart. Both had the same goals—improving the effectiveness and profitability of their production/distribution system—but they each felt that the other was acting in self-serving ways that damaged the industry.

Wal-Mart learned throughout the 1970s and 1980s that heavy discounting and price promotion of goods could boost market share,

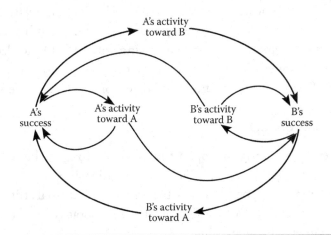

Figure 4.1 Accidental adversaries systems thinking model.

value, and improve profits. But price promotions created extra costs and difficulties for distributors like P&G. The Wal-Mart practice undermined P&G manufacturing, creating great swings in P&G's manufacturing volumes. The practices of each firm were intended to meet each firm's internal objectives but, as a partnership, each was always pointing a finger at the other claiming undermining practices. In responding more attentively to their internal objectives, the partnership fell short of optimizing its combined operational effectiveness.

While this pattern of behavior continued for years, attempts to reconcile and elaborate exactly what was happening was a difficult, if not impossible, order.

And so, this same pattern existed in the newly formed and maturing IT Project Office, among seemingly cooperative and optimization-oriented managers, who did not recognize the future implications of their antagonistic conduct. It is often not easy to discern or to admit that these behaviors take place among rational and intelligent groups who join their efforts to make a better condition within their groups.

But, as William Braun has suggested, the potential exists for archetypes to be applied to test whether the policies and structures under consideration may be altering the organizational structure in such manner as to produce the archetypal behavior. If PMO managers find this to be the case, they can take remedial action *before* the changes are adopted and embedded in the organization's structure.

Have you identified some recurring behaviors in relationships between your key PMO suppliers, vendors, partners, or other support groups, which can be limiting your attainment of PMO excellence?

Here are some prescriptive actions and seven action steps from William Braun in case you find candidates for accidental adversaries:

Prescriptive Action

- Revisit the original opportunity that brought the PMO parties together into a collaborative relationship.
- Use the archetype to identify the origin of adversarial attitudes.
- Renew the shared vision of the collaborative effort and commit to team learning.

Seven Action Steps

- Reconstruct the conditions that were the catalyst for collaboration and PMO success.
- Review the original understandings and expected mutual benefits.
- Identify conflicting incentives that may be driving adversarial behavior.
- Map the unintended side effects of each party's actions.
- Develop overarching PMO goals that align the efforts of the parties.
- Establish metrics to monitor collaborative behavior.
- Establish routine communication.

I don't want to leave you with the impression that this IT Project Office archetype produced a highly dysfunctional organization as it matured. Over a two- or three-year period, the management of the IT Project Office and the consulting firm realized and recognized the internal objectives of the other party, and actually began to discuss how they could support their own internal objectives while creating the fully functional IT Project Office that everyone envisioned at the beginning. Dialogue and continual realignment of values and vision were effective over time.

5

IDENTIFYING AND APPLYING LESSONS LEARNED

Lessons Learned are Experiences or Activities or Events that can result in an improvement to a Process.

Project Lessons Learned are Experiences or Activities or Events in a project that can be used to improve the project process or some subset of that process.

There are numerous examples of Lessons Learned in everyday life. For example, before Hurricane Irene hit the east coast, David Gregory, the moderator of "Meet the Press," asked the Federal Emergency Management Agency director, "What lessons have we learned from Katrina that would better prepare us for Irene?"

After Hurricane Irene hit the east coast, Governor Christie of New Jersey declared in a press conference "We are going to conduct an After Action Review of Lessons Learned to see how well we were prepared."

After every encounter with the enemy in Iraq, U.S. military commanders ordered a Lessons Learned exercise to prepare for the next encounter.

In the aftermath of the 2012 presidential election, Newt Gingrich declared in several talk shows that he would be spending the next seven months working on a Lessons Learned examination of the Republican experience in the election.

Lessons Learned may also be of a personal nature. Consider the scenario that, as you leave your home or apartment every morning, you use a key from your key ring to lock the door. Consider the situation in which several of your keys on the key ring are similar so that each morning you have to search for the right key by trial and error to lock the door. The same is also repeated in the evening when you return to your home or apartment. The result or outcome is that additional time is required to lock your home or apartment. You might term this your Ingress/Egress process if you were defining processes for your home life.

Now suppose you wanted to lock the door in 5 seconds but it took 10 because you had to search for the right key. This deviation between expected and actual might induce you to look for alternatives. One alternative would be to mark the right key clearly so you could find it the first time. Another alternative might be to eliminate all keys from the ring that looked similar to your home or apartment key as long as those keys were not essential to satisfy other key functions of your life. The lesson learned here would be that an improvement in Ingress/Egress process time would be possible if Alternative One or Two were adapted. The Process Improvement would be the implementation of either Alternative One or Two.

This might seem an extreme example to make a point, but the personal Lesson Learned could result in an improvement in the overall quality of life you experience.

In engineering, Lessons Learned exercises help to improve our engineering and construction standards such as in the Tacoma Narrows Bridge.

Slender, elegant, and graceful, the Tacoma Narrows Bridge stretched like a steel ribbon across Puget Sound in 1940. The third longest suspension span in the world opened on July 1, 1940. Only four months later, the great span's short life ended in disaster. "Galloping Gertie," collapsed in a windstorm on November 7, 1940.

The bridge became famous as "the most dramatic failure in bridge engineering history." Now, it's also "one of the world's largest man-made reefs." The sunken remains of Galloping Gertie were placed on the National Register of Historic Places in 1992 to protect her from salvagers.

The story of the failure of the 1940 Narrows Bridge and the success of the Current Narrows Bridge is a great American saga. When Galloping Gertie splashed into Puget Sound, it created ripple effects across the nation and around the world. The event forever changed how engineers design suspension bridges. Gertie's failure led to safer suspension spans we use today.

The Tacoma Narrows Bridge was a good example of a Lesson Learned. However, it can't really be considered a project Lessons Learned in the context of our discussion in this book, because the lesson that was learned occurred six months after completion of the project rather than during the project or at a project close exercise.

In the case of the Tacoma Narrows Bridge, engineers had failed to take into account some of the natural frequencies of oscillation that the bridge could exhibit when exposed to high winds, which typically occurred in that area during certain times of the year.

For more information, please see Appendix 7.

Exercises

1. Watch for news programs or summaries of current events in which the announcers specifically talk about Lessons Learned. Describe the context of the discussions in terms of value addition or placing blame for actions.
2. Describe to a friend an event from your experience where you learned a significant lesson about the situation and also your feelings at the time about the reflection you went through.
3. Do some additional reading about the events of the Tacoma Narrows Bridge collapse and the impact on engineering design.
4. Look for other examples of Lessons Learned from failed structures or vehicle design or financial institutions collapse or other such occurrences and describe the Lessons Learned.

6

What Is "Leverage" and How Can Project Managers Use It to Their Advantage?

Greek mathematician and inventor Archimedes said "Give me a place to stand, and with a lever I will move the whole world."

As a project manager, you have probably used the term "lever" in the engineering or physics context to describe a device that can be used to gain a "mechanical advantage" in a given scenario. It means that you can apply force, in varying amounts, to perform useful work. Likewise, "leverage," a commonly used word derived from the word "lever," means the application of any number of concepts to achieve some advantage in a given scenario for the person or group that is skilled in the application of the concept. Some forms of leverage might be an individual or group's position in an organization, a specialized knowledge, a unique piece of information, or a robust technology, etc.

A good example of technology as a "leveraging" variable arose in a New York Yankees baseball game with the Detroit Tigers. With Yankee Mark Teixeira on third base, the batter hit a ground ball to the infield that resulted in a throw from first base to home to stop a run from scoring. Teixeira slid into home plate and touched the base with his left hand while the Detroit catcher was almost simultaneously taking the throw from first base and applying the tag to Teixeira. The home plate umpire called Teixeira out, but Yankees Manager Joe Girardi disagreed. He challenged the call while his Yankee bench coach called the press box to get some other camera views of the play. Under challenge, the home plate umpire and umpiring crew chief consulted with the instant replay staff, whose use of camera technology has become an accepted practice in

Major League Baseball. The challenge by Girardi was upheld, and the home plate umpire's call was reversed. Girardi had used technology to leverage the situation. Before instant replay technology and challenge, the play would have resulted in an out for the Yankees, and no run scored.

Think of areas in your project management experience where you or a project team member, stakeholder, or third party has used position, knowledge, information, or technology to "leverage" a situation. How might you have prepared yourself or your team to "leverage" your outcomes and your project objectives?

The idea of "leverage" may be applied in an organizational dynamics connotation to describe how project Lessons Learned can be derived from seeing single projects as "events." In addition, a more "leveraging" connotation for project groups can be identified. This can help you make lasting changes in project or business processes by identifying "patterns of behavior" among a group of projects subject to the same project environment.

"Leverage," in this case, is insight about how project teams behave, how they organize themselves, what management principles and objectives they choose to follow, and what they value as being the "truth" for their direction.

Lessons Learned, whether they are developed by project managers or others engaged in process improvement, can also be "leveraged," because the "lessons learned" represent knowledge about some system or process that can be used to add "value" to the scenario. Feedback from performance or expectations regarding a system or process can improve the scenario which has broad implications for everyone involved.

Lessons learned from weather events, artistic performances, sporting or athletic events, elections, public officials' performance can all be used to "leverage" outcomes. The story is endless and only limited by your own imagination.

As we will learn later in the book, lessons learned may be influenced by facts, perspectives, and deliverables. Taking different perspectives seriously is an important aspect of lessons learned. Often perspectives are keys to "leverage" as lessons learned are implemented.

Timing is another variable of importance, particularly in scenarios which require a rapid response on the part of the actors involved. Business negotiation and legal issues are good examples here. Project management teams who need to deliver by a strict schedule can be "leveraging" agents in these scenarios.

The remainder of this book is a valuable story of project management lessons learned.

7

The Importance of Reflection and Changing Attitudes in Lessons Learned

By three methods, we may learn wisdom:

- First, by reflection, which is noblest;
- Second, by imitation, which is easiest; and
- Third by experience, which is bitterest.

Confucius

Reflection is the pause that gives a person perspective. Reflection turns experience into insight.

John C. Maxwell

Those of you who have seen the movie *The Ron Clark Story* already know about the remarkable efforts of a dedicated teacher in inner city New York who developed a learning atmosphere for his elementary students, which contributed to them excelling in the classroom at the highest level in every subject. Subsequent to Ron Clark's success in the New York schools, he visited every state to talk with students, teachers, and school administrators about what he had learned and how his students performed.

What he found in his journeys were the same characteristics that he had identified as success factors in his own classroom experiences. He found dedicated teachers and students and administrators everywhere who displayed some key attributes which, when tapped fully, created a learning experience that resulted in success and a learning environment that could not be denied regardless of the social setting or the prior experiences of the students and teachers.

When he wrote his second book *The Excellent Eleven*, he focused on the 11 characteristics of high-performing classroom, living, and learning environments that contributed to the success of a student. One of those characteristics was reflection. Ron used reflection to instill emotion in the students' experiences with their present-day studies. At the end of every major section of work, he made the students write down their impressions of what they had just experienced and how it affected them. What types of things were going on their lives at the same time, what emotions they felt as they mastered each subject, and what relationships they experienced. Many of the students remarked that, after reading their own reflections a significant time later than the actual events, they a amazed at the images the reflections created in their minds and the tendency to revisit those images as they experienced new and more challenging situations and environments.

Reflection is something we don't usually allow ourselves to experience because we are too busy getting on to the next task at hand, too busy hurrying to the next assignment that we don't pay attention fully to what we have created in the last assignment, too busy grappling with the next hurdle because it is there rather than analyzing why we felt a certain way about our work just completed.

Yet reflection is the very essence of what many of Ron Clark's students stated as being the most significant experiences they remember and the most often called-upon thoughts when they faced really formidable challenges in future years.

If you are a project manager or a project team member, make time to reflect in written form and at regular intervals what you feel about your experiences with past projects. What observations have you experienced when facing new hurdles, what paths of accomplishment have you taken to reach a successful plateau, and what thoughts would you share with another person who might be faced with a similar challenge.

The words of Confucius on wisdom will resonate in your mind over and over as you attempt new and more challenging tasks. Reflection will help you to tackle all things that seem formidable. Sharing those reflections with others will help cement relationships that are so valuable to the maintenance of the community of project managers and team members going forward.

Equally as important to project success is a change in attitude toward Lessons Learned.

I am sure all of us can remember Lessons Learned exercises in projects we were associated with, where the atmosphere was one of finding fault and determining who made the mistakes that the exercise highlighted. This finding blame seems to have been a prevailing attitude many project organizations expressed years ago about project Lessons Learned.

Slowly, over time, these attitudes have been changing. In my experience working with many project organizations, those organizations that embraced change were more likely to embrace Lessons Learned because they had adopted an attitude that Change Creates Opportunity.

Today, project organizations are much more open to project Lessons Learned exercises, and these exercises have provided value not only to the project organization and its customers and clients but also to the broader society in general.

Dr. Mehmet Oz, who hosts a successful television program that focuses on health and human wellness issues, provided another perspective with regard to the value of Lessons Learned recently. In one of his programs, he stated that one of every three second opinions that patients seek in their diagnosis of a condition results in an overturn of the original opinion. As he stated, think what value that could create for the medical community at large as well as society if that second opinion was shared with the doctor who provided the original opinion.

This attitude is a breath of fresh air for Lessons Learned. Indeed, the value of project Lessons Learned can be far reaching if the project lesson learned is documented in an actionable manner that improves the process of the organization.

Clark Howard hosts a radio and television program devoted to helping consumers with problems they encounter in everyday life. Usually, these problems are of a financial nature. The consumer has entered into an agreement for an article or service and the other party has not delivered or only half delivered the goods and services. The callers to the programs can always be assured that they will get good, sound financial advice and common sense about their problems. In a sense, the problems they are discussing with Clark Howard are Lessons Learned the hard way.

An action led to an outcome that was not the intended outcome or the expected result did not meet the actual result. There is a certain amount of risk taking on the part of the consumer who calls in, because his problem and often his befuddled actions will be broadcast on the air live. But the value to all consumers by this sharing of Lessons Learned and the sound advice from Clark Howard more than compensate for the caller's reluctance to share his problems. Indeed, Clark depends on Lessons Learned to fuel his consulting ability to help consumers.

Exercises

1. Describe a situation you had to analyze for your work and the "reflection" you used to identify the details.
2. Describe other situations in which reflection has benefited your thought processes about the details, outcomes, results, and behaviors.
3. Describe your approach to Lessons Learned. Are you a risk taker who is willing to share Lessons Learned with others as a means of helping each person who might have a similar problem?

8

THE BEST TIME TO DOCUMENT PROJECT LESSONS LEARNED

Note that the chapter title above says the best time and not the most convenient time.

The best time should be a time that will allow for reflection, feedback, and adjustment of any project assumption or other parameters that would contribute to the success of a project. It should be a time that will allow win–win solutions to be identified from issues with different viewpoints, as opposed to the compromise solutions that often occur in projects when a full look back and analysis has not been conducted.

In the past, project Lessons Learned were often modeled after the After Action Reviews from the military, in which a review session would be conducted after a military operation to capture Lessons Learned and positively impact the behavior of the team in future exercises. This was a convenient time (not necessarily the best time) for such reviews.

The After Action Review methodology was carried over to modern project management much as other practices are carried over from one discipline to another, without proper regard to what contributes the most to success in the future endeavors or in the current project at hand.

Instead of waiting until the end of your project, I suggest that you select intervals during the project for such reviews. These could correspond to stage gates if your project is organized in such a way, or they could occur at natural or major breakpoints in activities in the project schedule.

Documenting Lessons Learned at multiple points during a project allows a look back at the assumptions versus reality of the project and affords the opportunity to define new assumptions for the remaining portions of the project. Also, it allows time for reframing or asking the question "What problems are we trying to solve?" with the project.

How many projects have you seen completed where the project team, in looking back at what was accomplished, realized that they had addressed or answered the wrong question? Conducting project Lessons Learned at intervals throughout the project facilitates framing and reframing the major issues in the project.

Now that you've decided to conduct your project review at intervals throughout the project, the next question becomes "What framework should I use for conducting a project Lessons Learned session?"

The usual questions asked in a Project Lessons Learned exercise are as follows:

1. What was the expected result?
2. What was the actual result?
3. What is the deviation from actual to expected?
4. What is the Lesson Learned?

While this is a good starting point for capturing and documenting Lessons Learned, let's take this one step further.

I would recommend you look at the work of Roger Martin, Dean of the Rotman School of Management at the University of Toronto, to find a good framework for examining project Lessons Learned during the course of the project.

Over the course of about 15 years, Roger Martin studied how successful leaders think. Leaders from many different fields were interviewed and a thought pattern was discerned. Roger Martin termed this "Integrative Thinking," because it differs from "Conventional Thinking."

Among the features of "Integrative Thinking" that make it a good methodology for examining project Lessons Learned are the following:

1. Examination of more salient features of the project that might not have been considered when the original project was framed.
2. An integrative look at other issues that might impact the project so that a holistic view of the project and its impact on all stakeholders and the environment is considered.

3. An attention to architecture of the project and its major issues, which gives a good overall view of the systems dynamics involved in the project. This also provides clues to dependencies between your project's deliverables and those of other projects, i.e. the fact that projects *give* and *get* information and deliverables during the course of the project life.

4. A consideration of opposing viewpoints that does not acquiesce or dominate other viewpoints but rather takes into account the valuable features that contribute to a win–win situation rather than a compromise situation.

Let's take a simple example now.

Suppose your project has four distinct phases, each succeeding phase beginning at the completion of the previous phase in a linear fashion. Also suppose you want to conduct a project Lessons Learned session at the end of Phase One.

The sequence of activities you might follow in conducting this Lessons Learned exercise might be as follows:

1. Look at results from Phase One. Are there any assumptions that require revision before going into Phase Two based on the results of Phase One? Have you correctly framed the problem in this project based on the results from Phase One? Are there any other salient features that should have been considered in the project during Phase One that were not considered?

2. From a holistic standpoint and anticipating activities in Phase Two, have we learned anything in Phase One that would impact how we handle Phase Two (or for that matter, any later phase) activities?

3. Have we correctly planned the architecture of the project so that cause and effect of decisions and actions taken in Phase One can be clearly discerned in Phase Two and later phases? Are we certain of the dependencies between projects and the key gives and gets between or among projects?

4. How are opposing viewpoints concerning decisions and actions in Phase One being addressed? Are we taking the best features of opposing viewpoints to find the final solution or do we still need to seek compromise when opposing

viewpoint clash? How will we proceed to a win–win solution for the project outcomes so that stakeholders are satisfied with the project outcomes?

In conclusion, look for opportunities to conduct project Lessons Learned sessions and to document the lessons when it makes sense to conduct them.

The real value of project management is when Lessons Learned are fed back into project schedules and plans, and positively impact project team behavior and the resulting project decisions. Success of projects is more assured if Lessons Learned are taken seriously and every team member takes ownership of both the identification and sharing of project Lessons Learned.

9

THE ACTUAL COST TO YOUR PMO FOR NOT CAPTURING AND SHARING PROJECT LESSONS LEARNED

When a recent panel discussion focused on Hurricane Katrina's devastation of New Orleans, the commentary on "Meet the Press" stated that it was the largest man-made disaster in U.S. history; not the largest natural disaster.

Why?

Because at some point in the past, a large (failed) project was undertaken to reinforce the New Orleans levee system. This project was supposed to reinforce the levees so that they could withstand the floodwaters of anticipated hurricanes and storms. Unfortunately, the levee system failed during Katrina.

A new levee system was installed by the Army Corps of Engineers. There are many Lessons Learned, resulting from the previous levee failure during Katrina, as well as many years of data from previous storms and computer simulations. These Lessons Learned are currently being addressed by the design of the new levee system.

What is the actual cost of failure to capture and share project Lessons Learned? Aside from the human cost of storms like Katrina, what is the actual project cost that is incurred by not capturing, documenting, sharing, and institutionalizing project Lessons Learned? How can we get a manageable and actionable handle on the real contribution of project Lessons Learned on saving future project costs?

The answers to these questions obviously depend on many factors: the complexity of the project, the number of impacted systems, the number of dependencies of project information with other like systems, etc. How can we get a handle on this type of information, and of what value would it be if we were to understand and apply it?

43

I once studied with a professor whose favorite expression was *Analysis Is the Essence.*

It did not really dawn on me what that statement meant until I encountered some business situations where bad decisions resulted in a failure to meet objectives, such as on time, on budget. In these cases, it seemed to me that the logical sequence of events should be analysis followed by rational thought followed by decisions to proceed followed by actions.

We all know that while it is easy to recommend to others courses of action, or specific rationale, or well-thought-out research findings, it is very difficult for others to actually follow-up, and to take the recommended courses of action.

Why is that? I believe that everyone has a tendency to believe that if they did not think of an idea themselves, then that idea is not of value to their ongoing, daily processes. And they may also be biased, and emotionally involved in the decision, so that their rationality does not shine through. As is often said, you can clearly lead a horse to water, but you can't make him drink. It takes motivation and capability.

People decide to take courses of action based upon recommendations from others based on the credibility that they attach to the advice-giver and the usefulness of previous directions from that person. Leaders become true leaders when they continually disallow their own thinking in favor of the more qualified thinking of their peers and associates; they have learned over time that their own thinking provides merely one perspective of a scenario that really demands many viewpoints to assess, understand, and take action.

So, how do you get people to embrace project Lessons Learned—first, as a logical step in the project management process, and second, as a rational, thought-based process to provide information for future decisions about project work?

In the course of assisting project teams and Program Management Offices (PMOs) with developing project Lessons Learned, I have often encountered a resistance to taking the time to develop and capture Lessons Learned and to share this information with others. Emotional entanglement—as well as a lack of motivation in the sense that no immediate reward will be forthcoming (and perhaps that negative consequences may ensue)—often dictates the action or inaction. And I am sure that, if you are actively engaged in project work in a PMO, you will have encountered the same.

So let me suggest another tactic.

There is a cost to be borne by the PMO for not capturing and sharing project Lessons Learned.

To get a simple model for this cost, let's assume a model that is often used to get across the point that introducing changes at various key points in a project introduces additional cost to accommodate those changes. And when the need for those changes is recognized, impacts how much of a cost results.

If a project has, for example, four distinct phases, and if a change is introduced during the first phase that costs $10, that same change may cost $100 if introduced during the second phase, $1,000 if introduced during the third phase, and $10,000 if introduced during the fourth phase.

Now, suppose that a project Lesson Learned is identified in phase four, and that project Lesson Learned could impact a change at that point, if the original need for a change had been identified in phase one, it would only have cost 0.001 times as much.

Suppose two or three project Lessons Learned could be identified for every project. Thinking in an integrative manner to identify where projects could have been improved at previous project phases can deliver real cost savings. The point here that you should grasp is not whether the savings is 0.001 times the final cost of the change, but that this perspective can yield significant savings to any project, no matter how complex or simple. Train yourself as a project manager to think in these terms and you will always be able to find significant opportunities in Lessons Learned to benefit both your company and your reputation as an efficient and highly skilled project manager.

Hard dollar reductions are the result of project Lessons Learned.

What is the situation in your PMO? Are project managers willing to share project Lessons Learned? Does the organization have a process for documenting and sharing project Lessons Learned with future project teams?

Exercises

1. Think of a project in your experience in which a late design change caused unnecessary additional resources or timing to complete. Could that design change have occurred at a previous phase of the project? Try to estimate the cost to the project of not making the change earlier.
2. Think of a project for which the original assumptions were not revisited during the project. Did any of the assumptions change resulting in a change to scope or deliverables? What is the impact of assumptions on the outcomes of projects?

10

APPLYING PROJECT LESSONS LEARNED AS A BEST PRACTICE FOR YOUR ORGANIZATION

Among the themes that I have developed so far are as follows:

1. *Why* it is desirable to conduct project Lessons Learned reviews at specific intervals in the project, such as Phase Gates, rather than waiting until the project Close Process.
2. *What* the actual cost to the Program Management Office (PMO) is for not developing and sharing project Lessons Learned.
3. *How* PMOs can make project Lessons Learned a Best Practice in their organizational and business context?

I predict that we will soon see PMOs focusing on project Lessons Learned as a primary focus rather than a secondary focus (as has been the case in the recent past). More organizations are seeking to close out projects in a more formal and documented manner, and project Lessons Learned is an excellent framework to follow.

Here are some other items I see contributing to this trend:

1. The need to include risk management in every aspect of project planning and execution. Risk can be included as a variable in the project Lessons Learned framework, especially if applied in a project Lessons Learned schedule that calls for a review at the Phase Gates at the end of each project process.
2. Project Lessons Learned will eventually be captured and stored in new systems (such as new versions of the application Microsoft Project) so that the information can be treated as just another piece of performance reporting information for a project.

The discipline of project Lessons Learned is important for a number of reasons:

First, it contributes to a continuous process improvement environment in project organizations.

Second, it increases the knowledge base of project teams.

Third, it positively influences the total cost or timing of projects going forward.

Fourth, it improves quality.

Fifth, it improves collaboration among teams.

Sixth, it improves the project environment.

Seventh, it provides insights in risk management.

Capturing, documenting, and sharing project Lessons Learned is a valuable exercise in every project group, because it forces the project community to reflect on its outcomes versus actions and behaviors in project team situations.

Project managers who fully experience the project process learn and acquire truth, knowledge, decision-making skills, and good judgment. There are three primary methods by which project managers may learn these lessons:

First, reflecting is the preferred method because it results in the highest value to the project manager. Reflection means focusing attention on or studying an event or outcome to understand its origin and root causes as they apply to new project situations.

Second, imitating other project managers' documented, shared experiences is the easiest method by which project managers may improve their skills. "Imitation" means to behave in a manner that mirrors the "best practice" actions or behavior of others.

Third, repeating his or her own bad experiences and unplanned or poor outcomes may also result in the project manager developing his or her skills, although this method causes the most pain and, in most cases, creates the least value addition.

These concepts paraphrase Confucius' fifth-century BC quote concerning wisdom and Lessons Learned, from a previous chapter. They relate concepts of behavior, actions, outcomes, experiences, pain, ease, value addition, and knowledge.

Why is it that project managers refuse to accept the reality that it is more painful to keep repeating the same mistakes in their projects, rather than to learn and benefit from the experiences of others?

Lou Tice, of the Pacific Institute, was a great leader and trainer in the field of developing human potential and achieving personal goals. Among other things, he taught two principles of personal growth and development:

1. People act in accordance with the truth, as they perceive it to be.
2. People move toward and become like that which they think about.

As Lou Tice suggested, project managers who act as if project Lessons Learned can have no positive impact on their future success act in accordance with their perceived truth that project Lessons Learned aren't valuable. Similarly, many organizations have been reluctant to require their project managers to take the time required to reflect upon their completed projects and document their project Lessons Learned, despite the fact that most Project Management Body of Knowledge (PMBOK) practices suggest that project managers properly close-out projects with an after-action review and documentation of project Lessons Learned.

However, I believe that this reality is beginning to change. Many companies have begun to take project Lessons Learned more seriously and are interested in closing-out projects with documentation, preserving the knowledge created by the project and the experiences of project participants.

On the other hand, what do project managers want to do more than anything else when they successfully complete a project? Those of us who have observed this behavior over time can tell you that overwhelmingly project managers want to get on to that next great assignment, that next great challenge, and that next great project. Rarely do they want to pause and reflect upon what they have just accomplished or what the organization could gain if they documented and shared their project management experiences.

So, what should be the driving force for properly documenting and sharing project Lessons Learned?

We all know that most organizations now recognize that there are certain Best Practices—in both their project management processes and their business context—which they employ over and over again. This is to be expected; when an organization experiences a successful outcome using a key Best Practice, the organization is likely to have a successful outcome in the future if it employs that same Best Practice again. Often, these Best Practices are specific to that organization's culture, and they fit into the project process naturally in the course of executing projects. Indeed, many organizations are employing Best Practices intuitively now. Few companies, however, are adept at recognizing and employing their own Best Practices.

Just like Best Practices have become—no pun intended—Best Practices within many companies, shouldn't PMOs look upon project Lessons Learned as having the same potential to lead to success in their project work?

Here is a process and framework for looking at project Lessons Learned that will allow the project Lessons Learned process to become a Best Practice in your PMO:

Ask yourself: what would constitute a capability-based system for capturing and sharing project Lessons Learned?

1. Fact-Sorting Process—There must be some process or mechanism for sorting out the Facts in stories, experiences, and anecdotes versus Assumptions.

2. Candidate-Review Process—There must be a recognized review process to identify candidates for project Lessons Learned.

3. Genuine and Authentic Feedback Process—There must be a willingness on the part of project managers and project team members to speak directly, concisely, and with conviction about project events and lessons. This involves a risk-taking attitude that only comes from developing an internal capability in the organization to acknowledge that project Lessons Learned add lasting value.

4. After Action Review Question Process—There must be a review process that addresses the following questions:
   • What were the Expected Results from the action or behavior of the project team?

- What were the Actual Results from the action or behavior of the project team?
- What is the gap between Actual and Expected?
- What are the Lessons Learned to be captured, shared, and documented?

5. Internal Knowledge System or Process—There must be an internal knowledge-management system devoted to storing project Lessons Learned documentation so that project managers may easily retrieve and apply the lessons contained therein to new projects.

6. Focal Point Caretaker Process—There must be a single person or a focal point group who is the coordinator or caretaker of the project Lessons Learned process and knowledge-management system, so that he or she can analyze the documented Lessons Learned to identify any broader Lessons Learned that may be applied to the policies, processes, and procedures governing the organization's project management processes.

Once you have mastered these basic elements and gain some experience in applying the process to a number of projects, you can begin to add some sensitivities. For example, you can relate project Lessons Learned to the risk of developing a new technology concurrent with the project within which the new technology is being applied. At the outset of the project, you can establish a plan to prove out the technology as the project progresses. A lesson learned can then be documented in terms of the risk of the new technology being proved out successfully during the project. Such a scheme could introduce concepts such as controllable and uncontrollable risk. Controllable risk could be associated with those portions of the technology prove out, where there is a high probability of success.

Likewise, you can look at project Lessons Learned at the end of each major phase of your project and apply some integrative thinking principles. This allows a reexamination of original assumptions for the project and sets the tone for good project planning for future project phases.

Where does your PMO stand on closing out projects?

Exercises

1. What are some Best Practice processes that your project organization has identified and followed consistently?
2. Describe a current process that you are utilizing in your project work, which has the potential for becoming a Best Practice process for the organization.

11

UNDERSTANDING AND USING THE NEW PROJECT FRAMEWORK

As we have stated several times in this book, project managers inherently want to get on to the next project so they can "manage" and exert an influence on project outcomes, which in turn impact overall strategies of organizations. They wish to leap from a project Close directly to project Lessons Learned by recalling from their own experiences what seemed "significant" to the project—not necessarily what was both "significant" *and* "actionable" in terms of being converted to an input for a Continuous Process Improvement Process (Figure 11.1).

The problems that arise from project managers leaping to project Lessons Learned without a framework for guidance are several:

1. Project managers don't always focus on high-priority events that are related to project outcomes and results.
2. Project managers only present one perspective of project events.
3. Project managers often express their hurried Lessons Learned in language that is far from actionable.
4. Project managers can present a highly biased position.

The Framework I present here is intended to provide a mechanism for closing out projects, documenting project Lessons Learned that are actionable, and contributing to continuous process improvement through the actionability of the lessons documented.

The framework focuses on Significant Events from projects, which have created deviations between Expected Results for the project and Actual Results. We call this deviation a gap.

Once Significant Events have been examined closely enough to become candidates for Lessons Learned, then we examine whether

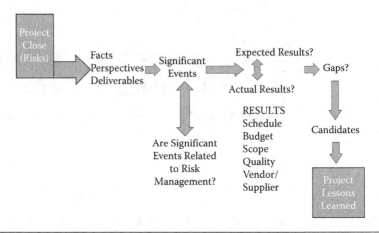

Figure 11.1 Project Lessons Learned Framework.

the Lessons Learned from these candidates would actually produce actionable results. Actionability is defined as capable of being incorporated as a process improvement in a Continuous Process Improvement Loop for a process. It also includes the criteria that the Lessons Learned be written and expressed in such a manner that someone who was familiar with the project community and the project environment could reasonably make the process improvement change. This implies that the organization has the capability to make the change, which is a key criterion in itself. Often project organizations do not have this capability as they begin pursuing project Lessons Learned, and they must develop or acquire the skills and competencies to effect such process improvements (Figure 11.2).

So, let's examine the specifics of the framework.

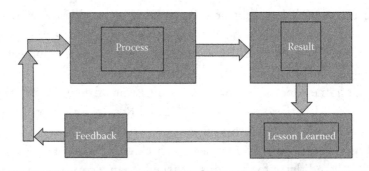

Figure 11.2 Continuous Process Improvement Framework.

Identifying Significant Events

There are three key areas of interest when developing Significant Events for project Lessons Learned exercises:

- Facts
- Perspectives
- Deliverables

Facts

Facts are those recorded or recordable specifics about a project that are irrefutable. What was the start date for the project? What was the finish date? Who were the project team members? Who were the Stakeholders and Customers? What change orders were recorded, and how did they change the scope of the project and resulting outcomes from those of the original scope?

Facts serve to place stakes in the ground for further investigation of the events of the project. Without facts, we have nothing to use to describe events.

Perspectives

Perspectives are those viewpoints held by project team members about what happened in key scenarios during the project. Lou Tice once said that "people act in accordance with the truth as they perceive it to be." This was a guiding principle of his teachings, and it forms the basis for our focus on perspectives in project Lessons Learned.

Every project team member, every stakeholder, and every customer has their own perspectives regarding what happened or transpired in a project, and sometimes few agree on their perspectives, at least at the beginning of such discussions with regard to Lessons Learned. The project manager must gather and review the various perspectives that project personnel carry with them regarding the scenarios in projects.

Often, these perspectives will focus on Significant Events in projects that were nonplanned for during the initiation and planning stages. These Significant Events are what the project manager is most interested in as he seeks to identify candidates for project Lessons Learned.

Project managers must often reconcile differing perspectives that project team members carry with regard to the events and scenarios in a project. There is nothing worse than reaching the end of a project Lessons Learned exercise and having two project personnel disagree on the major events or what transpired in a specific project scenario.

Project managers must recognize that they will encounter bias in soliciting various perspectives of project scenarios. They also have to recognize that they themselves introduce bias into the procedure. They must be aware of confirmational bias, in which a project team member may express a perspective of a scenario, which basically reinforces an established belief or opinion that they have held throughout the project.

What are some good examples of perspectives? In the 2012 London Olympics, for example, a reporter asked a swimmer from China about the success of the Chinese team in the Olympics after the first week of competition. The Chinese swimmer said that, in his opinion, other teams from other countries were trained to qualify for their country's team or just trying to qualify to compete in the Olympics, whereas the Chinese team had been trained to win the swimming competition. This difference in perspective was important to the team in the way it prepared and in its expectations for a finish.

Another connotation of perspective in this case of identifying Significant Events is the perspective of the project manager with regard to the events of the project. Among the various perspectives that can be examined are technology perspectives, resource perspectives, process perspectives, political perspectives, environmental perspectives, geographic perspectives, market perspectives, and any perspectives that are peculiar to a given type of project. These same categories of perspectives may be in play in the risk management focus, because certainly there are technology risks, resource risks, process risks, political risks, environmental risk, geographic and market risks, and any other risks peculiar to the specific project.

The project manager must take care to examine each of these perspectives, if they make sense for a given project, to really ascertain the Significant Events. Significant Events often occur during breakdowns in the function of the process, resources, technology, political, environmental, geographic, and market practices. For example, if resource skills and competencies are insufficient to develop the deliverables according to the project plan, a Significant Event occurs.

Deliverables

Deliverables are the planned outcomes of project work. As such, they are often associated with milestones, which are points in time when deliverables or portions of deliverables are completed by the project team and are ready for input to the next phase or stage of a project. Deliverables are usually tangible artifacts from projects like reports, or a product or process that is used to produce value for the end users or customers of a project. Deliverables can also be processes, value addition functionality of base deliverables, or new project activities.

Scenarios in projects that produce deliverables are often captured in Lessons Learned exercises because they contribute to the overall history the project creates. Often, focusing on the actions of the project teams that led to the development of the deliverables will help identify Significant Events that created deviations in Expected versus Actual Results that the project team had to overcome to create the deliverables.

Another aspect of deliverables is the activity or sequence of activities that contributed to the development of the deliverable. The quality of the activity in terms of whether it contributed the right resources, or number of resources, or technology, at the right time and the right skill level for deliverables development, often leads to identification of Significant Events for examination as possible candidates for project Lessons Learned. In other words, the quality of the deliverables is directly proportional to the quality of the activities that produce them. Therefore, it pays to look closely not only at the final deliverables but also the activities or tasks that produced them when looking for Significant Events for project Lessons Learned.

Identifying Significant Events Related to Risks

If the project group has an active Project Risk Management Plan in place, then potential Significant Events have already been identified as part of the Risk Management Plan. This is a key link between this Framework and Risk Management and sets it apart from other frameworks. When identified at the early stage of projects, potential Significant Events or Risks are those events that, if they occur, can result in an adverse outcome for the project.

In my experience working with project groups, those who have an active Risk Management Plan will more than likely develop a robust project Lessons Learned process.

Mitigation plans are often defined in a project group that has an active Risk Management Plan. If a risk is triggered, then certain actions will have been defined by the project team to mitigate the risk. Someone is assigned the responsibility for making sure the Mitigation Plan is implemented so that the result of the risk can be lessened as much as possible.

This is a strong point about the framework presented here—the fact that it integrates well with any Risk Management Plan that the project group uses that focuses on potential Significant Events that might be termed risks. Those organizations with an active Risk Management Plan for projects are already 90% of the way to having a project Lessons Learned Framework that can be enhanced into an actionable project Lessons Learned process.

Identifying Actual versus Expected Results

For each Significant Event identified for a project through examination of Facts, Perspectives, and Deliverables, and with reference to the Risk Management Plan, ask the following questions:

> What was the Expected Result?
> What was the Actual Result?

Results in this case are the measures of how your organization associates project progress with:

- Schedule
- Budget
- Scope
- Quality
- Vendor and Supplier Management

Identifying Gaps

Examine the gap between Expected and Actual Results for each of the Significant Events. Often the Results in "Identifying Actual versus

Expected Results" section can be focused on Schedule, Budget, and Scope, although many organizations also choose to look at Quality of results and Vendor and Supplier performance in defining gaps in results.

Identifying Candidates for Lessons Learned

An examination of Significant Events, and the Gaps between Expected and Actual Results, will lead to identification of Candidates for project Lessons Learned.

A rule of thumb applies here that we must document: If a deviation between Expected and Actual Results would be reported in the normal periodic reporting cycle used by the company, then the candidate associated with that deviation is probably *not* a project Lesson Learned.

The rationale for this rule of thumb is that, if a deviation would be reported in the normal periodic reporting cycle, chances are that the outcome was planned for in the project, and the deviation is the result of normal operational deviations, and *not* the result of a Significant Event. Significant Events are *not* planned for in the course for the project. They are significant because they occur without being planned, and because they create gaps between Expected and Actual Results.

Preparing the Project Lessons Learned Template for Documentation

The project Lessons Learned template is a simple document with a table focusing on four questions:

- What was the Expected Result?
- What was the Actual Result?
- What is the Gap?
- What is the Lesson to be learned?

Other information can be captured and documented in the Comment sections, such as how the Lessons Learned will be stored and shared with the organization, and what specific actions will be taken to ensure that other project teams are made aware of the Lesson Learned.

Qualifying Candidates with an "Actionability" Criterion

Ask the questions:

- Is this Lessons Learned "actionable?"
- Is this Lessons Learned capable of being integrated into the process as a process improvement?

How a project Lessons Learned is documented in terms of its ability to be understood by others in the project community who understand the business context, and the project environment will determine whether it is truly a Lesson Learned. Could another competent project community member pick up the description of the Lesson Learned and, given the resources and tools to enable them, implement the process improvement? That is the true and lasting criteria of project Lessons Learned. They must contribute to a Continuous Process Improvement Framework for the organization to fully satisfy their place as a project Lesson Learned (Figure 11.3).

The Bottom Line

It is easy for project managers to make some qualitative remarks about what needed to be improved in their projects after they complete the project. The problem with this approach is that it represents only one point of view. It is clearly biased and contains no qualifying criteria

Figure 11.3 Project closeout and Lessons Learned Framework.

that stand the scrutiny of a larger project organization that desires to implement an "actionable," "repeatable," "consistent" project Lessons Learned process.

The framework, however, provides a proven mechanism to create Lessons Learned that are Actionable, and that can be implemented in a Continuous Process Improvement Framework (Figure 11.4).

Aspects of Facilitation of Project Lessons Learned Exercises

In working with project groups as they implement project Lessons Learned frameworks, it has become apparent that many project groups are questioning whether the project manager should be singled out to develop the facilitation capabilities that such a project Lessons Learned framework calls for to be truly effective and of value to the organization. Many project organizations that wish to implement this Project Lessons Learned Framework have identified a select group of project personnel to facilitate such Lessons Learned exercises across the project organization. One group I recently worked with was a Project Controls Group, whose members are required to look out over the projects in their portfolio and develop recommendations for how all the projects in the portfolio can improve their performance and delivery. This Project Controls Group has taken on the task of equipping several key members with the necessary skills and competencies to facilitate the project Lessons Learned exercises for the entire project organization, rather than burden each project manager with the need to develop competencies.

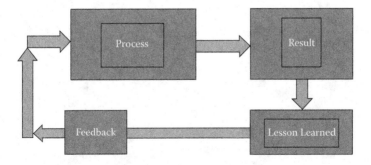

Figure 11.4   Continuous process improvement using project Lessons Learned.

Exercises

1. Listen for conversations in your project group wherein two people express different perspectives on a project scenario. Record some of these observations.
2. Look at the activities from two projects that produced similar deliverables. Describe the quality of the deliverables in terms of project team activities.
3. In your own terms, define actionability.
4. Recall an event from one week ago and describe the details of the event to a friend. Recall an event from one year ago and describe the details of the event to a friend. Repeat this same exercise with the same two events about a month from now. How accurate are your details about the event one week ago? One year ago?

12

RECOGNIZING AND USING DIFFERENT PERSPECTIVES

When I teach project managers about project Lessons Learned for the single project case—that is, when a project manager identifies, documents, and shares Lessons Learned from a recently completed project—I emphasize three areas upon which they must focus their attention to determine Significant Events for Lessons Learned. The three areas are (1) Facts; (2) Perspectives; and (3) Deliverables.

The end objective of a project Closeout and Lessons Learned exercise is to determine actionable changes that can be made to basic processes to improve performance of projects and the organization in total. Actionable changes need to be agreed to by the organization's participants so that they are committed to the changes and work to sustain the changes over time. And someone in the organization needs to be assigned the role to make the process changes, so that the actionable Lessons Learned fit easily into a continuous improvement framework for the organization.

To provide better understanding of perspectives, let's give a definition and an example.

Perspectives are different viewpoints that people may feel or express about a situation or an action or an event that represents their interpretation about the truth of the situation, as they perceive it. An example would be the following exchange recently between David Gregory, moderator of the NBC News Program "Meet the Press," and a Republican Candidate for the Presidency.

Mr. Gregory: Mr. Candidate, isn't it true that none of your colleagues in the Congress have endorsed your Candidacy for the Presidency?

Candidate: The truth, Mr. Gregory, is that I have not asked any of my colleagues from the Congress to endorse me yet. I will at the appropriate time.

You see from this exchange that each person expressed a viewpoint about the same situation or potential action or event that represented their own interpretation of what was true for them in their business, social, or political context.

Sometimes, perspectives are reconcilable and sometimes they are not. Two parties may continue to disagree about the truth of a given situation. In this case, they cannot agree whether it was a Significant Event or how significant the event was to the overall outcome of their work. Reconcilable perspectives are important in agreeing upon what really happened in a given situation.

Because project participants bring many different viewpoints to projects as to what was significant, and as to what really took place in the project, each of the project participants possess what I term perspectives.

Perspectives are viewpoints that capture the truth as perceived by the viewer. However, people act in accordance with the truth, as they individually perceive it to be. Project participants often "perceive" different outcomes and actions in projects and disagree about what really took place. That is why I advocate starting with Facts, i.e. the statements and data that no one can refute.

Timing is also important for gathering and processing perspectives. The closer to the project Lessons Learned exercise the perspectives were documented, the more they will reflect what truly happened in the project. If we allow much time to pass from project Close to the capturing of Lessons Learned, the perspectives will often be colored by other experiences that the project participants have been involved with after completion of the project.

A principle of Louis Tice's is that "[p]eople act in accordance with the Truth as they perceive it to be." Their definition of a project's Significant Event may be different from yours if they see a different Truth in the actions or outcomes of the project. Reconciling different perspectives, and gaining agreement about the Truths of a project, is often critical to gathering Significant Events and then qualifying them as Candidates for project Lessons Learned.

Project managers and other project team facilitators must be adept at sorting out the feelings that project participants, sponsors, steering committee members, and subject matter experts express about Truths and Outcomes in a project.

Even experienced project managers often find it difficult to sort out and deal with the various perspectives that project participants bring to the table to discuss as part of a project Lessons Learned exercise. Identifying project Lessons Learned and sharing them with others are the major steps toward building an internal organizational capability to develop actionable project Lessons Learned that can contribute to a Continuous Process Improvement Framework for a project team or organization.

Another aspect of perspectives is reframing. Project managers and facilitators must be adept at reframing positions to bring out the relevant facts and viewpoints that make sense in identifying Significant Events for project Lessons Learned.

I encourage anyone truly interested in becoming a "curator" for their project environment, in terms of capturing, documenting, sharing, and perpetuating project Lessons Learned, to practice the flow from Significant Events, to candidates, to full Lessons Learned, by actively involving themselves in the reconciliation of perspectives in Lessons Learned exercises.

You will be happy that you took the time to focus on identifying and reconciling perspectives because it will provide you with new insights into interpreting events, actions, and feelings on the part of project participants. It will also help you to record those Truths about projects that can lead to more in-depth insights into project performance and ongoing project success.

Challenge yourself in the next project Lessons Learned exercise that you conduct or facilitate for a project team to recognize and appreciate the different Perspectives and their contributions to fully understand your project environment and context.

In most cases, lessons learned exercises proceed from start to finish quickly. They may be part of a project Closeout session at the end of a major project. Participants in Lessons Learned exercises, therefore, form their views on Facts, Perspectives, and Deliverables at a "point in time." Facts are those pieces of information that most people recognize as irrefutable or may reflect a generally held attitude or belief by the population in an organization. Perspectives may differ from participant to participant in Lessons Learned exercises. We have discussed the need to reconcile these perspectives in some cases in other sections of this book. Actionable lessons learned from project Closeout sessions are usually implemented quickly by organizations to capitalize on the improvement in performance of their basic processes.

There are cases in which Facts, which were assumed to be irrefutable or commonly agreed to in the course of a project, may actually be impacted by Perspectives (or Research) that provides new information on the Fact in question. A new book by Lynne Olson entitled *Last Hope Island: Britain, Occupied Europe and the Brotherhood That Turned the Tide of War* tells the story of Britain's role in World War II. For example, for many years, it was considered a Fact that Britain played an "isolationist" role in World War II, and was only reluctantly drawn into the war after the United States and Russia joined the war after Pearl Harbor. In actual fact, Winston Churchill brought a new attitude into the Prime Minister's role, and invited the leaders of the occupied countries of Europe to come to Britain after their countries were invaded by Germany. Churchill was very proactive, and it led to cooperation of the European countries, which eventually resulted in the formation of the European Union (EU). The author offered perspectives on the roles of the European countries in World War II as they directed their efforts from Britain, and described how the Polish forces flew airplanes for the Royal Air Force, and how the Norwegian merchant fleet helped the English survive when the Germans were sinking so many British cargo vessels. This is a good example of how Perspectives can impact Facts or Beliefs that are widely accepted in an organization as the Truth. Needless to say, there is much subjectivity in this approach.

In an actual example from a project, a Fact identified during a project Closeout session was that the budgeted expense for the project was met at $4.0 million. (Budget and actual were $4.0 million.) Several project participants noted that $200,000 of Development Budget funds had been used to staff the project with resources according to the Project Charter terms. If these funds had been expensed in the Project budget, the Actual expense would have been $4.2 million. The impact on decision making and Lessons Learned for this project was that all future project expenses would be authorized by the Project Charter from the Project Budget.

In the final analysis, the behavior of nations, business organizations, project organizations like PMOs, and governments is essentially similar. We understand that their performance is dictated by the structure they have put in place to guide their organizational and business processes and their daily operations. Lessons Learned must be an integral part of our life experiences as we interact with the environment around us.

13

Dilemmas and Choices Faced by Project Managers

As project managers and Program Management Office (PMO) practitioners, we continually strive to improve our performance by reflecting on those areas where we excel, and critically review areas where we could create more desirable outcomes when faced with similar circumstances. When facilitating the project Closeout and Lessons Learned process, the project manager faces many choices and dilemmas on his journey to actionable project Lessons Learned.

Dilemmas are one area of conflict where we can all improve our performance.

Dilemmas arise from internal or external conflicts between goals, values, perspectives, and points of view. In this chapter, let's examine some elements of the conflicts that give rise to dilemmas for project managers. As you will see, dilemmas provide learning and growth opportunities for project managers to review and choose a course of action. John C. Maxwell, who is known as a present-day guru of leadership, has often been quoted as saying that "leaders have choices and when they make those choices, the choices in turn make them." As leaders, project managers are often faced with those same choices in the form of dilemmas.

Here is a story from my life that may provide a helpful illustration of a dilemma:

During the summer between my freshman and sophomore years in high school, I collected insects. Not because I had a great interest in insects, but because several rising juniors had informed me that the sophomore biology courses required a leaf collection one term, and an insect collection the next term. Those students who were unlucky enough to get the insect collection assignment in the winter months often could not find good specimens of the most common insects in our geographical area. Hence, to get good marks in the course, we needed to start a collection as soon as possible so that we could be assured of getting a good representative cross-section of insect types.

I rigged up an insect net by bending a wire coat hanger for a frame and using an old sheer curtain my mother had discarded from a window treatment. The mesh was sheer enough not to let out any insects but transparent enough that you could clearly see your catch. So, armed with my handy insect manual and my rigged net, I was the scourge of the neighborhood and nearby streams and ponds looking for specimens.

I was lucky that my family took a driving vacation trip from our home in North Carolina to Florida's Gulf coast during that summer because I was able to find several varieties of Gulf Fritillary butterflies that were native only to that area. I thought that would give me a decided advantage with the judges of the insect collections. Several people had also informed me that bright lights would attract insects during the evening hours, and under a lighted sign, I was lucky to snare a rhinoceros beetle on that trip.

When I returned home, I made a trek early each morning to an all-night laundromat about a mile from my home to see what moths and other nocturnal insects might be left over from the night before. Most of these treks yielded very little, except for an occasional small moth like a sphinx moth, which has a bright colored pattern on its wings. Then, one morning as I walked up to a large screen at one end of the laundromat where the exhaust fans seemed to roar on incessantly, I stopped in my tracks when I saw something at the corner of the screen that was both large and colorful. I had never seen anything like it, and I had poured through that insect manual dreaming of catching something exotic that would really "wow" the judges.

It was a greenish-blue color with a wingspan that must have been at least four inches from side to side, and it had curved tails on its wings extending back from the body and symmetrical about the centerline of its body. It must have been six inches long from top to bottom. What was it? So, I pulled out my handy-dandy insect manual and I started to leaf through the pages. It only took me three or four minutes to realize that I was looking squarely at a Luna Moth.

Now, if you have ever seen a Luna Moth, you will know that its beauty and sheer size are the most distinct characteristics. Why do they call it a Luna Moth? Naturally, because it is out when the moon is out!

A million thoughts ran through my head. I did not have much time to think about the consequences of my find. Any time now the sun would be high enough that the Luna Moth would loosen its grip on the screen and be gone. My first reaction was that this was going to be the greatest insect specimen that the school had ever seen, and I was thrilled to think that I would be applauded as the student who uncovered the specimen.

But, then a second thought ran through my mind. What right did I have to capture this beautiful creature and inject it with alcohol to preserve it for my collection?

I had to hurry and decide. On the one side, my mind argued that since I had devoted so much time and effort to this project, I needed to achieve the best possible outcome and to share it with everyone. On the other side, my mind argued that my collection with its smaller moths, butterflies, beetles, and dragonflies would do just fine without it.

Looking back on that moment today, I really did not have the option to take a picture. Digital cameras didn't exist. Back then, pictures were taken when there was a deliberate need to take pictures, and disposable cameras were not available in every drug store. Spur of the moment yielded no camera readily available for a picture. The only camera I could hope to put my hands on was a clunky camera my family used on vacation and it was in our house a mile or so away. So technology was clearly a variable that I was not fully aware of at the time.

I faced a dilemma. My decision was to capture this insect for my collection. The Luna Moth was clearly an example of an insect in the insect manual and it qualified as a specimen acceptable to the teacher in satisfaction of this assignment. To this day, however, I often rationalize my decision to capture this Luna Moth, because I had no idea if the biology teacher would even have accepted a picture in place of a real specimen. From what I heard from those juniors, the assignment was to collect specimens—not take pictures of them.

We are faced with dilemmas in our work and our personal lives every day. How we resolve them is a personal matter. But we should all consider that everyone faces dilemmas, many of which are never revealed to anyone else.

Cordell Parvin, my good friend and colleague, provides training and coaching for lawyers. When we discussed dilemmas one day, he said that, in the legal context, one dilemma he faced was "whether to take a client/case when I knew I would be paid a lot of money but I did not like what the client was trying to accomplish. Another dilemma is when I have had a client who only wanted a lawyer who would agree with him. I call it a 'yes' man. In both instances, I resolved the dilemma by not taking the matter or client. I know that lawyers are supposed to represent clients who are bad people or who have done bad things. But, for me I could not totally separate my feelings from our concept that even the worst of us is entitled to a lawyer."

Project managers are no exception—you have probably faced dilemmas on several occasions.

Have you ever stopped to think about the crucial decision elements and the choices that help you to resolve dilemmas? Consider the following dilemmas that project managers may face:

Scenario One: A SAP project manager is planning his budget for the next SAP project. He knows that other SAP projects have typically overrun their budgets because of the need for additional resources and project work in the data conversion phase. He also knows that the PMO is controlling budgets closely for upcoming projects, so he is reluctant to include a full amount for any data conversion resources that may cause the budget to seem inflated versus previous SAP budgets. How is his planning for the project affected by these different perspectives?

Scenario Two: A project manager who is in charge of a design team to provide a major component for a larger assembly has identified a risk in the use of the component; namely, at lower temperatures than the assembly has been subjected to thus far, and which are not normally encountered by the assembly in its usage pattern, the component may lose its elasticity and become more rigid, thus potentially compromising the performance of the assembly. He knows that the next proposed application for this assembly will likely be in the lower temperature range. He has alerted the design manager, but the design manager refuses to inform the contractor of the potential flaw. His rationale is that every assembly to that point in time has performed flawlessly, and there is no need to think that the major contractor would desire a redesign if the risk of a failure was very low. He asks the project manager to confirm his analysis regarding the identified risk. Does the project manager confirm that low risk or continue to raise a red flag about a potential failure?

When facilitating project Lessons Learned exercises or facing project dilemmas such as the earlier sample scenarios, what are some key conflict and decision elements that project managers should consider?

1. Timing

     In the case of the Luna Moth, since I had a limited time in which I could capture the moth, timing was of the essence in forcing a resolution to the dilemma.

2. Goal or Outcome

     Often, conflicting goals are an issue. There may be, for example, conflicts between personal goals and organizational goals, between the goals of two individuals, and between internal personal goals and externally defined peer group goals. The experience of the individual project manager frames the project manager's determination as to what are the possible choices. For example, in the case of the Luna Moth, having only the input from former students, I believed that the only way to fulfill the assignment was to actually collect (rather than photograph) the insects.

3. Perspective or Frame

     I have often stated in this book that people act in accordance with the truth, as they perceive it to be. Right versus wrong is often based on the truth that an individual defines for himself in the world. Choices are then defined by those truths.

4. Technology

     In the case of the Luna Moth story, did I really at that time believe there was a technology choice to be made between taking a picture and harvesting the specimen? Or, did my mind and experience inject that into my story as I recalled the incident based on my years of experience in facing other dilemmas and choices that had a variety of technologies available for deployment?

5. Interpretation of the Facts

Two individuals experiencing the same scenario may view the events and actions of the participants in entirely different ways based on their experiences, value systems, and what they consider the truth.

6. Reality or Wishful Thinking

When reflecting on past events or experiences, we often inject our own stories into the scenarios because we are continually telling ourselves stories based on our observations, biases, values, and what we each consider reality.

Dilemmas provide us with a playground for testing our viewpoints versus others' viewpoints.

Roger Martin, Dean of the Rotman School of Management at the University of Toronto, has written a great deal on the topic of "Integrative Thinking." Integrative Thinking is a framework for evaluating conflict in scenarios, and was detailed in this book in Chapter 7. I encourage project managers, when faced with new dilemmas, to look upon them as opportunities to grow and develop their own integrative thinking framework. Think of some dilemmas you have faced in projects and share your experiences with others who have faced similar dilemmas. You will be surprised by how many different viewpoints and interpretations will surface when you discuss your past dilemmas with others.

As I have alluded to before, John C. Maxwell has outlined the impact that choices make on leadership development. The choices that project managers make in the course of their projects, in turn, make them. Choices like responsibility, accountability, integrity, compassion, and value-based decision making can impact not only other project managers and the PMO practitioners around them but also other individuals in the organization, the organization itself, and those with whom the organization interacts.

Project Lessons Learned exercises provide project managers and project teams the opportunity to develop their competencies and capabilities in a number of areas, which in turn make them more valuable to the organization and to the project community.

14

Identifying Valuable Candidates for Project Lessons Learned

Even the most experienced project managers can sometimes feel that they have difficulty in identifying candidate events for Lessons Learned. To a project manager in the day-to-day project battle, any deviation might look like a Lesson Learned candidate.

Certainly, a Lesson Learned candidate should be an event that is significant and needs to be shared with the project community. Remember our rule of thumb—if you have a project event that represents a deviation between expected result and actual result and will be reported in the normal performance reporting cycle or process, then it is probably not a Lesson Learned candidate. For example, if an event causes a deviation in actual cost versus budget schedule or in actual schedule versus budget schedule, and that event will be reported in the normal performance reporting cycle, it is not a project Lesson Learned candidate.

Now, let me give you several examples of what I would consider good candidates. Those of you who utilize Enterprise Resource Planning (ERP) and especially SAP systems will recognize that one area that causes organizations great concern during projects is data conversion. In fact, when I worked with a major Program Management Office (PMO), every SAP project we completed that involved significant data conversion caused us to exceed schedule or cost or resources. Data Conversion is one of those topics that can have diverse subtopics (like scrubbing). So, I wrote a project lesson learned about Data Conversion in SAP projects, because we wanted future SAP project managers conducting Data Conversion to plan accordingly for resources, competencies, required time, and expense to complete Data Conversion.

In this case, Data Conversion represented a significant event that we wanted to highlight to all project managers for future projects.

Another example involves Technology Prove-out. If a project involves proving out a new technology during the course of the project, then a lesson learned should be written that relates the risk involved with introduction of the new technology and the mitigation or monitoring process used by proving out the technology. In this way, the risk throughout the project can be divided into controllable and noncontrollable risk elements and the Lesson Learned will stand as a benchmark for future projects that involve technology prove-out.

In other words, significant project events that relate risks and outcomes, which are outside the day-to-day project business process or routine, are most likely to be candidates for project Lessons Learned.

Now, to keep project Lessons Learned to a manageable number for a project, it is important for the project manager to coach his team on how to identify project Lessons Learned. But there is no rule that says you can only identify, say, for example, 10 project Lessons Learned for any given project. That is up to the discretion of the project manager, his team, and the stakeholders. Interpretation and good judgment should prevail here.

Once Lessons Learned have been identified and documented using the template from Appendix 1, there are a number of options for sharing with the organization and storing the Lessons Learned for future use by project teams.

Sharing Lessons Learned

Once project Lessons Learned have been documented using the template, project organizations must choose which methods they will use to share lesson learned among the project community and future project managers.

In my experience working with PMOs, one of the best methods for sharing project Lessons Learned is through meetings such as Breakfast Forums, in which the project manager reviews project results as well as Lessons Learned. I have found that those project managers who have a certain risk-taking attitude often step to the forefront and share their project Lessons Learned most freely. And those same project managers often become leaders of the PMO as the PMO evolves and matures. Likewise, if your organization holds regular Sponsor or Stakeholder meetings to review upcoming and past projects, a review of project Lessons Learned often creates excellent dialogue about what can be changed in the organization and its structure to alleviate future significant events in projects.

Storing Lessons Learned

If your organization has a Knowledge Management system in place, it makes an ideal setting for storing project Lessons Learned.

Some organizations use a set of collaboration tools such as Microsoft's SharePoint or Lotus to make Lessons Learned available to a wide range of project personnel. Some later Microsoft products are beginning to incorporate Lessons Learned repositories for easy use by project teams and for examination by "curator" roles in the organization to identify patterns of behavior among several projects or project teams.

In my experience, as set forth earlier, I have used Breakfast Forums as a vehicle to share Lessons Learned across the project community. The project manager for the project usually shares these Lessons Learned, and the sessions are videotaped and offered through the company Intranet for others to view.

If a Lesson Learned is particularly significant, or one that the organization has not learned well over many projects, a special case can be made to document the lesson learned in a form shared at every level of the organization. Such was the case we discussed in the Data Conversion case study in this chapter. This particular lesson had been identified in several ERP/SAP projects, and the only way to reinforce the organization's desire to do a better job with Data Conversion was to write and document it in such a way that everyone in the organization, not just the project organization, was made aware of the issues and the resolution.

The Intranet is a particularly effective tool for making the organization aware of recurring themes in projects for which Lessons Learned have been recorded repeatedly with little success in a process improvement that will have long-lasting value to the organization.

Within the business context of each project organization resides the optimum way of sharing project Lessons Learned. Project managers and PMO managers should use their imagination where possible to ensure that the Lessons Learned are captured, documented, shared, and remembered.

Please check out the three Case Study Project Lessons Learned scenarios in this chapter. Each scenario uses the template from Appendix 1 to demonstrate how the Lessons Learned would be documented for an organization.

Case Studies for Project Lessons Learned

The following case studies are meant to provide an opportunity for the reader to understand how the various steps in the Framework complement each other and contribute in total to "Actionable" project Lessons Learned. I have used these cases in actual training courses, and they have provided much insight to those who are serious about project Lessons Learned as an input to a continuous process improvement mechanism for project groups.

Case Study 1: Project Lessons Learned Scenarios Systems Development

Background: A systems development project was completed by an IT PMO with an estimated duration of 16 months. Project business requirements included the applications to be developed and the functional specifications to be met. A Steering Committee was assembled, consisting of stakeholders from IT, the functional business group, and other subject matter experts. During the data conversion stage of the project, the project manager determined that he did not have the appropriate number of resources or the right composition of resources. Additional resources were identified at significant additional cost to the project. The project was completed in 19 months at a cost increase of $3 million.

Project Closeout Discussion: The project manager was informed by several other project managers that his definition of data conversion was too broad and that he needed four other subcategories to better define skills and resources needed.

These were as follows:

1. Old data cleanup
2. Data scrubbing

3. Data translation

4. Data compatibility with new application

The deviation from expected was an additional three months duration and $3 million. Alternatives for handling future projects like this were discussed. It was agreed that, not only was this a candidate for Lessons Learned, but also that it needed documentation for future project managers. Facts and perspectives were discussed so that everyone was in agreement with the events and the implications to the project.

(This was the second such project in this PMO in which a project manager had not planned for the needed resources and competencies for data conversion. At that point, no one had seen the pattern of behavior.)

Systems Development Project—Project Lessons Learned Summary

What was the Expected Result?
1. Project would be completed on time.
2. Project would be completed on budget.
3. All functionalities of new systems/ application would be provided.

What was the Actual Result?
1. Project was completed three months late.
2. Project was completed $3 million over budget.
3. Data conversion stage of project was identified as the one significant reason for deviation from expected result.

What is the Gap?
1. Gap between expected and actual was due to inadequate planning of data conversion stage.

What is the Lesson to be Learned?
1. All data conversion stages of projects will be subdivided into old data cleanup, data scrubbing, data translation, and data compatibility with new application.
2. Project manager will review all new data conversion stage estimates with IT Governance Committee during Planning Stage.
3. Documentation will be stored in Microsoft SharePoint and Intranet.
4. A Breakfast Forum will be conducted with the project manager reviewing the Closeout discussion.

Comments

1. Examine project plans, assumptions, deliverables, risk management plans, business case, and financial case for the specific events.

1. Analyze actual performance versus expected performance for significant events.

1. For each significant event, define the gap between expected and actual in as much detail as you can.

1. For each significant event, summarize in detail the lessons to be learned.
2. Cite risk, new technology prove-out, and other key factors.

---

*Case Study 2: Project Lessons Learned Scenario New
Construction and Installation of Equipment*

Background: A PMO completed a project that involved construction and installation of a new monitoring system for oil pipeline flow. To simulate the flow conditions, the vendor installed a prototype of the flow system in his laboratory so that all specifications could be assured in design so that he could have a good demonstration flow device to show the client. The development cost for the prototype was borne by the vendor.

At the time of certification of the new flow device in the client's facility, the device did not operate as planned and provided erratic readings of flow rate as well as interrupted flow occasionally. The PMO demonstrated this to the vendor, who insisted that the installation was the same as the prototype in the vendor facility that the client had signed off in development as meeting functionality and specification.

The project was scheduled for completion in March 2011; however, because of the lack of functionality of the installed device, it was now June 2011. The vendor still insisted that the installed device was exactly like the prototype and that the poor functionality must be due to the client's erratic pipeline systems and not due to his new flow device. The client insisted that the vendor perform or the contract would be terminated.

The two parties decided to install the prototype in the client facility and the new device in the vendor facility for comparison. This incurred additional expense and it was now July 2011. The new device in the vendor facility operated as intended, and the prototype in the client facility operated more erratically than had the original installed device.

The client held internal meetings to determine further steps. It was discovered that a malfunction had occurred in a valve upstream to the new flow meter installation, which contributed to the poor performance of the new installed flow device. Client Management was concerned that the installation of the new flow device had contributed to a backflow of pressure that affected the valve operation. Client Management made the decision to replace the upstream valve and reinstall the new flow device. At the time of testing, both the upstream valve and new flow device were evaluated as a system and performed to specification. Three additional months had elapsed and $4 million additional expense incurred.

Project Closeout: Facts and perspectives were discussed at the closeout meeting. It was determined that no one monitored the upstream valve during and after the time of installation of the new flow device, so it could not be determined that the valve failed to operate correctly. It had last been replaced five years before, and the most recent *significant* maintenance on the valve was determined to have been three years before. The vendor made a claim for $2 million for additional expense due to testing and reinstallation of the new flow device and the vendor's resource time for the troubleshooting.

(A similar occurrence in another valving and low system was recorded by a separate team when replacing a valve at a later date. They referred to the Lessons Learned from this event for direction.)

New Construction and Installation of Equipment—Project Lessons Learned Summary

---

What was the Expected Result?
1. Project would be completed on time.
2. Project would be completed on budget.
3. All functionality would be met.

1. Examine project plans, assumptions, deliverables, risk management plans, business case, and financial case for the specific events.

What was the Actual Result?
1. Project was completed two months behind schedule.
2. Project incurred additional cost due to vendor.
3. Functionality was met.

1. Analyze actual performance versus expected performance for significant events.

What is the Gap?
1. Gap between expected and actual was due to lack of total system test for new installed flow.

1. For each significant event, define the gap between expected and actual in as much detail as you can.

What is the Lesson to be Learned?
1. New system testing procedures and specifications will be introduced when any modification is made to the flow monitoring devices in the facility.
2. Engineering and Project Process Review teams will be informed of the action.
3. Documentation will be provided in the MS SharePoint system.

1. For each significant event, summarize in detail the lessons to be learned.
2. Cite risk, new technology prove-out, and other key factors.

Comments

Case Study 3: Project to Install Fire Suppression Equipment at a Port

(This case is provided without a solution so that the reader can test his or her skills at identifying Significant Events and Lessons Learned.)

Background: A project was completed at a major port. The project consisted of supply, installation, test, and adjustment of a firefighting system to replace an existing system.

The port was located at a major East/West logistics point. Over time, the port handled larger and larger vessels and the requirements for fire suppression were accented. Several fire-related incidents could have resulted in damage to the larger ships or, worse yet, complete shutdown of the port operations. The Port Authority approved this project as a major strategic initiative. Fire suppression systems were installed at several points in the port due to its size and vessel movements so that the project was aimed at one of the largest suppression systems for replacement.

The scope of the project consisted of civil works for the installation of water and foam solution pipelines, construction of pump and foam solution houses, mechanical works for the installation of the system components, electrical works for the system, electronic works for the supply and installation of the communication and control system, and other works that are necessary to facilitate the system operation, and as part of these works, the water discharge and foam solution tests were included.

A major overriding objective for all projects conducted by the port was maintenance of operation of the port as a first priority. A less communicated objective but still a concern in every project manager's mind was cost control. This often resulted in resources dedicated to projects that were a minimum to meet scope, timing, and cost objectives or, in some cases, shared resources with a specific technical support group.

A number of design changes were introduced during the course of the project. The project team realized that they were designing a world-class fire suppression system for the expanding port. Pressure requirements as well as pump and motor capacity were examined closely and adjusted to meet new definition requirements throughout the project.

The motors for the new pump system were designed by a top-tier manufacturer/supplier in a country distant from the port. Stringent specifications were supplied to the manufacturer concerning voltages of operation and other operational specs. As a result of these stringent specifications, several potential suppliers dropped out of the competition so that one single supplier emerged as the source.

During an on-site field component test of the new fire suppression system, it was discovered that the motors were not operating at the voltage specified by the design team. A project team meeting with management revealed that, as a cost-containment measure, no design engineer was permitted to travel to the manufacturer's site for observation of tests and review of design specs. A review of the design certification showed that the manufacturer had supplied the motors with a voltage that did not conform to design specs or to the certified rating. Respec'ing the motors resulted in a 6-month delay in delivery of the new motors.

During another system test, a safety switch was inadvertently left on and the pumps and motors operated for over 24 hours without any monitoring. This resulted in damage to the pumps that had to be repaired.

In several project team meetings, inspectors voiced a concern that they had been asked by supervisors of major contracting firms on-site to direct the contract workers in meeting certain scope requirements so that they would assuredly meet the design criteria specified in the project.

At project completion, additional costs of $10 million had been incurred. The project was delayed 12 months from its original scheduled completion date.

A project Closeout meeting was convened to discuss and document project Lessons Learned. Objectives of the meeting were to document project Lessons Learned.

What steps should the project manager have made in preparation for the project Closeout meeting?

What project Lessons Learned should be documented?

What are some risks in the port operation?

Use the project Lessons Learned Template below to record your solution.

What was the Expected Result?	1. Examine project plans, assumptions, deliverables, risk management plans, business case, and financial case for the specific events.
What was the Actual Result?	1. Analyze actual performance versus expected performance for significant events. 2. See chapter on selection of "candidates for Lessons Learned."
What is the Gap?	1. For each significant event, define the gap between expected and actual in as much detail as you can.
What is the Lesson to be Learned?	1. For each significant event, summarize in detail the lessons to be learned. 2. Cite risk, new technology prove-out, and other key factors.

Comments

15

USING THE PROJECT FRAMEWORK TO THE BENEFIT OF ENTERPRISE RISK MANAGEMENT

Most project organizations in their early stages of development probably do not have active risk management capabilities in place. It is usually after some experience with developing project outcomes from many projects that project organizations begin to associate risk with outcomes and plan accordingly. Feedback from the customers, stakeholders, audit groups, or the project community itself begins to focus the project organization on the need to develop competencies and capabilities in the Risk Management area. Taking risks into account in defining project plans and devoting resources to Risk Mitigation Plans are actions that project organizations begin to pursue as they rapidly mature.

Risk Definition

Every initiative has risk elements. Every project has elements of risk. Risk is defined as an Event, which, if it occurs, can result in adverse outcomes for a process or activity. Project Risk can be defined as a Significant Event in a project, which, if it occurs, can result in an adverse outcome for a project.

Risk Characterization

Risk is usually defined by two parameters: Likelihood and Impact. The likelihood of occurrence is the probability that the risk will occur. The impact is the effect the risk has on the project or process if the risk is triggered. These two parameters are often plotted on axes to show the combination of Likelihood and Impact.

Risks occur for ongoing operations as well as for projects. When combining the parameters Likelihood and Impact, four quadrants are apparent. Usually organizations address the High Impact/High Likelihood cases when developing Mitigation Plans. However, there are some cases where Risks outside the High Risk/High Likelihood quadrant can be significant. Take, for example, the BP Gulf of Mexico oil spill in 2010. In this case, the Likelihood of occurrence was thought to be low because of the high reliability of the blowout preventer used in the drilling process. However, the Impact was thought to be quite high such that, if the risk was triggered, the potential effect on the environment or community could be quite high. Indeed, that is exactly what happened. This High Impact/Low Likelihood case is often not addressed in project work.

As I mentioned in a previous chapter, there are various risk categories similar to our perspectives discussion that must be examined: technology risks, resource risks, process risks, political risks, geographic and market risks, etc. It is important for project managers to recognize that risks can be identified for each of these categories.

Project groups usually develop Risk Mitigation Plans for High Likelihood/High Impact risks. They also identify Triggers for the risks so that a complete characterization of the Risk can be addressed in the Project Risk Management Plan.

Because project organizations that have an active Project Risk Management Plan in place focus on potential Significant Events in risk definition, these organizations are closer to developing good project Lessons Learned Processes than other project organizations who have no active risk management plan in place.

Project Risk Examples

One of the most unusual discussions of project risk I have been involved in occurred while I was facilitating two three-day courses in project Lessons Learned for the Panama Canal Authority Construction Division in July and August 2011. The Panama Canal Authority was engaged in a $5 billion Canal Expansion Program set for completion in 2014, the Centennial of the opening of the original Panama Canal in 1914. The course participants were project managers, contract administrators, project engineers, inspectors, contract specialists, and other personnel. During our group discussion to identify significant project risks, the project teams might encounter in the Canal Expansion Program, the topic of unknown site conditions continually surfaced.

When I questioned what unknown site conditions meant, I heard the following story. In 1933, the U.S. Army Corps of Engineers was called into Panama to add another set of locks and expand the canal. The Corps worked until 1939 on this assignment and then they were redeployed to the World War II effort. However, much of their work in excavation, concrete work, and preparation of the site was left unfinished. As much of the land grew over with forest and trees, the work was obscured. So, that is why today, when contractors are called into action in certain areas of the Canal Expansion work, one of the risks is unknown site conditions.

Many PMOs and project organizations employ third-party services such as contractors and vendors to complete projects. Among the major risks with using third parties is the contractor resources risk. This risk can have several dimensions. For example, does the contractor or vendor possess the right skills and competencies to complete the scope defined by the project? In some cases, it may be that a contractor has performed admirably for all previous projects he has been involved in. When new project opportunities become available, the contractor may be awarded work based on his previous excellent performance. However, it may be the case that the contractor has now spread himself too thin in terms of actual numbers of resources available to carry out new projects. This is a very common mistake many project groups encounter.

In the original Panama Canal Project, which was finally completed in 1914, one of the major risks not addressed at the beginning of the project efforts was disease. No one considered the malaria and yellow fever carried by the mosquitoes in the region to be a significant factor in the project's progression. The impact of malaria and yellow fever on the human resources used in the project was devastating in terms of maintaining a level work force during the project.

See Appendix 4 for a summary of the Panama Canal risk management story.

16

THE TREMENDOUS IMPACT OF ROLE MODELS ON PROJECT MANAGEMENT LEADERSHIP

When I was a teenager, I walked into our family room one evening and found my father on his hands and knees in the middle of the floor. Around him were four flip charts, and he was drawing with crayon freehand on each of the four flip charts.

"What are you doing?" I exclaimed.

"You remember last week when I was in Detroit for 4 days on that Service Training trip?"

"Yes. I wasn't sure which topics you were covering, but does this have any relation to that?"

"Yes. I am preparing some charts to explain the new transmissions we are introducing in our tractors to our service managers and our field organization. This is really exciting stuff, but it takes a picture to make it come alive."

"Didn't the company give you any material to train your service people with; pictures and descriptions of the new transmission?"

"Well, of course they did. But I did not think those handouts really conveyed the ease of operation and the full leverage that exists with the new transmission. That is what impressed me the most."

As he proceeded to fill the four flip charts with diagrams and words, I began to see what a "trainer" my father really was. I never associated his job as service manager in the southeastern District of Ford Tractor as a training job, but he clearly did. I was amazed that, by the end of the drawing that evening, when he explained the new transmission and its features to me, I actually understood what he was saying. His pictures and words combined the right thoughts and pictures in my mind to make sense of this new engineering feature.

Now, I have to reflect on this situation today. Is this why I am a good "trainer?" Is this why I use words and pictures and diagrams and flow charts to express my ideas and concepts to my audience? Did I see someone else in action who I copied in my later life as I developed into an excellent trainer? Yes. Decidedly, I believe that role models are the most effective means of experiential learning that we can have. The lasting outcome of having role models in our lives is to provide living, responsive models for our development and our maturity.

I had never really considered my father to be a "trainer" before. He was a "manager" of a number of other individuals who reported to him in the organization. There are several principles at work here. Lou Tice provided these principles in his teachings on developing potential and reaching for own heights of success.

First, people move toward and become like that which they think about. Having role models to view and interact with brings us closer to action that resembles the role model's actions and outcomes. That is not a literal statement, of course. It really means that we "imitate" much more than we would think we might in our lives.

Second, people act in accordance with the "truth" as they perceive it to be. When a role model presents a "truth" to us that matches our own value systems and beliefs, we adopt the mannerisms and processes that the role model exhibits.

What do good role models do that sets them apart from ordinary people?

I believe that "role models" set the standard for the way a discipline or a field of endeavor is carried out.

First, role models are passionate about the field of their discipline.

Second, role models do more than the minimum required to get the job done. They have a passion for conveying to other people more than exists on the surface. Role models are often "risk takers," but "calculated risk takers." They often rise to leadership positions in groups.

Third, role models are not pretentious. They don't try to show how much more they know or how much more they can convey. They are "genuine" in their approach and that "genuineness" shows through to others clearly.

Fourth, role models view "teaching" as part of their job, part of their mission in their field.

Fifth, role models can provide extremely effective experiential learning for project managers. Because role models can provide feedback and answer questions about their actions and resulting outcomes, they can provide the perfect "simulation" for view.

With the exception of mentoring—a one-to-one relationship between two persons—more than any other type of learning— classroom, team experience, case studies—role models are the most desirable of all leadership training routes.

Let me provide a few examples of good project manager role models from my experience. There was a project manager with whom I worked at ConocoPhillips whose assignment was to merge three companies occupying the same geographic region into one company that used SAP as the financial and management reporting system for the company. Before he assembled a project team or talked to the other principal stakeholders in the merger, he traveled around to all the company locations and talked to employees individually, getting feedback and comments on what had worked well in the past, what processes should be maintained, what processes should be abandoned, and how each person felt about their role in the new company to be formed.

At the time, some IT Shared Services Management questioned whether he should have taken the trip, but rather, whether he should have gotten on with the task at hand of organizing his project team since a deadline loomed in the not-too-distant future for the merged company to be active. What he did, however, was to successfully gain commitment from everyone at all levels of the organization, while reassuring them of their place in the new organization. A real What's In It For Me example, so to speak. When he formed his project team, he included many people from each of the three companies who advised and commented quickly on actions of the project team. Everyone saw this as a great example of a role model at work solidifying the success of his project and the company going forward.

Another example is my introduction of project Lessons Learned Breakfast Forums to the IT Shared Services Program Management Office (PMO) organization. We had not had a formal project lessons learned process in place to that point in time. I knew that commitment to such a program would only be solidified if I gained the confidence of a few "risk-taking" project managers to make it happen. One project manager stepped forward and volunteered to be the first project manager to address the Breakfast Forum with her project lessons learned. We videotaped the sessions and they became a hit on our intranet. The project managers who stepped forward and participated in the program became instant role models for other project personnel.

Perhaps someone has influenced your actions and behaviors without you really realizing the effect they have had on your thinking and your actions. Look for role models in every discipline you are involved in. They are worth the time and effort. They are the essence of the new project leadership. Chances are that many role models you have identified in your daily work use Lessons Learned as essential input to improving their processes.

17

FACILITATING A CLOSER CONNECTION

Lessons Learned, Risk Management, and Knowledge Management

Knowledge Management is a process that cannot thrive in a vacuum. (Well, actually, no process can survive in a vacuum, but that's beside the point.) Knowledge management is a discipline that promotes an integrated approach to identifying, capturing, evaluating, retrieving, and sharing all an organization's information assets. These assets may include databases, documents, policies, procedures, and previously uncaptured expertise and experience in individual workers. Knowledge Management is a "process" that must thrive on digesting inputs to its base, storing information, providing information to other processes and activities, and continually being assessed to see how it is measuring up. These inputs can be as simple as operational data from a firm's ongoing day-to-day work. It can be event-driven lessons learned information from a completed project. It can be transactional information from the firm's accounting and reporting systems. Data and Information Elements are the primary inputs to the Knowledge Management system. We will discuss more about their structure and origin in the organization later.

As a process, Knowledge Management has been characterized in its organizational setting by a Knowledge Management Maturity Model (KMMM). Several such models exist. In general, the KMMM defines how an organization, its people, processes, and technology are positioned at different levels of maturity. The highest level of maturity describes a self-actualized organization where continuous process improvement and learning are the standards of each day's operations.

In general, the KMMM has been designed after the Capability Maturity Model, which was developed in the 1980s for information technology organizations. We will talk more about "maturity" as we investigate the Knowledge Management Process and its interaction with other processes.

The "value" of a Knowledge Management system resides in how it is used by the various groups and clients it serves. The value of the process also resides in how well it collaborates with other processes. Since the firm defines success in many ways, the value depends on the myriad of ways that a Knowledge Management system contributes to that success.

A Similar Process for Comparison

To fully understand the interactions among the various processes of this book, I have chosen another similar process to provide an example. This process I call the "Complete Scientific Investigation Process." This process contains three elements: Theory, Experiment, and Modeling. In scientific study, an investigator wishes to use all three of these elements to provide a complete and accurate look at the phenomenon he or she is studying.

If you reflect on your elementary and middle school days when the teacher announced "Science Experiments," he or she often said "Choose a Hypothesis and then conduct an Experiment to either prove or disprove the Hypothesis." The idea was that relating this Experiment to the Hypothesis provided a true understanding of science from the viewpoint of elementary or middle school students. Many students were left with the impression that this "hypothesis/experiment" was what "science" was all about and quickly abandoned the idea of studying science in later education. Those of us who progressed into real scientific investigation later on found that it took more than a Hypothesis and an Experiment to really understand science. In fact, it took understanding and delving into Theory and relating the Theory to Experiment. It also took Modeling to help us understand how Theory and Experiment are related. So I am introducing a new concept called the "Mature Scientific Investigation Process" to mean that Theory and Experiment complement each other, that Theory and Modeling complement each other, and that Modeling and Experiment complement

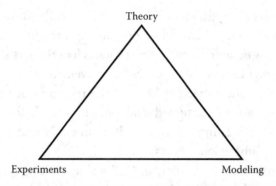

Figure 17.1   Scientific method complementary relationship between variables.

each other. This means that new developments in any of the three elements can have an effect on the other two elements (Figure 17.1).

As an example of the way this Mature Scientific Investigation Process works, take the example from 1953 in which James Watson and Francis Crick discovered the structure of DNA. Using theories of how molecules joined and bonded, along with X-ray experimental data from other scientists at laboratories in England, they proposed a model or structure for DNA that matched the information from the theory and experiments. So they were able to completely determine the structure and composition of a DNA molecule with these three elements.

Many people who have studied this discovery have concluded that the real accomplishment of Watson and Crick was to piece together five or six seemingly unrelated pieces of information into a DNA structure that obeyed the Theory, Experiment, and Modeling elements. It is this type of thinking that integrates several theories and disciplines, which we are trying to emulate with Knowledge Management structures.

Now, what does that have to do with Knowledge Management?

The Lessons Learned Process

What has been the history of lessons learned processes when implemented?

Many Knowledge Management systems rely on input from organizational Lessons Learned processes. Lessons Learned are experiences from projects or operations that can be used to improve a process.

Many project practitioners believe that it is difficult to implement a Lessons Learned system: How do you capture and share Lessons Learned? How do we ensure that everyone values the Lessons Learned process to provide actionable process improvements?

All these questions need to be carefully thought out and resolved, and the mechanisms designed and put in place before a Lessons Learned system is launched. Inattention can easily lead to failure and the failure of subsequent efforts.

As we have discussed earlier, an "actionable" process creates a result that anyone in the organization who is knowledgeable about the processes can implement. Therefore, it must be documented fully and well stated to be understood.

We covered this in a previous chapter.

The Risk Management Process

"Risk" is defined as an Event or Activity that, if triggered, may lead to adverse consequences for the organization. (To be complete, there is also upside risk in which advantageous outcomes for the organization may occur, but, for purpose of our discussion here, I am referring to downside risk.) As discussed earlier, an analysis of risk usually involves two concepts: the likelihood of occurrence of the risk and the impact if the risk does occur. These two dimensions create a matrix with four quadrants. Risk may occur from operations in an organization or from project work. When organizations analyze risk in this fashion, they usually develop Risk Management Plans for those risks identified in the High Likelihood of Occurrence and High Impact quadrant of the matrix.

By way of example, recent problems with ships in the Carnival Cruise Line have heightened an awareness of design factors in the affected ships. After the first occurrence of a ship that was adrift at sea without propulsion, the investigation yielded the fact that some of the Carnival ships were placed in service before 2000. In 2000 or that time frame, the law changed to require a redundancy in some propulsion systems so that, if a failure occurred in the main propulsion, a backup system would be activated. In all likelihood, this design factor may have been the result of Risk Management practices being applied more stringently to the design of the Carnival ships. Although I do not know if this is the case, the Occurrence/Impact matrix for such a "Loss of Propulsion" risk would certainly have been High Impact.

Another example is the BP Horizon Platform oil spill, which is a good example of risk management factors at play. The failure occurred in the blowout preventer on the oil well at a significant depth in the ocean or Gulf of Mexico. Now, if we had looked at this from a risk perspective, the Likelihood of Occurrence would have been classified as low because the blowout preventer had been very reliable in its operation in the past. However, the Impact would have been quite high because of the amount of oil potentially in the gulf from an event.

Having a robust Project Risk Management Plan in place helps to facilitate the project Lessons Learned Process, which has been identified by a number of observers as potentially problematic in its management. The Lessons Learned process is a key input to Knowledge Management.

The Data and Information Element Process

Data and Information Elements for Knowledge Management do not appear from the sky. Data and Information Elements are created in the organization at any point where information is created or developed that needs storing, classification, and sharing. Data and Information Elements may be Event Driven, Transaction Driven, Condition Driven, or Program Driven. Examples of these are given as follows:

Event Driven
    Operations
    Project Lessons Learned
Transaction Driven
    Financial
    Reporting
Condition Driven
    Environmental
    Weather
Program Driven
    Created by organizational or business processes such as project
    Management

For example, in the area of health care knowledge management, there are both "event-driven elements" and "transaction elements."

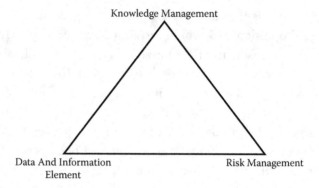

Figure 17.2   Data elements relationship.

For example, a cardiologist may order an angiogram for a patient and that is certainly "event-driven" information, but the identification and reporting of results is transactional (Figure 17.2).

**A Better Connection between Risk Management
and Knowledge Management**

What we are really doing here is developing a relationship between Data and Information Process, Risk Management Process, and Knowledge Management Process. Risk Management may be applied to the other Data and Information Elements similar to the way it is applied in the Lessons Learned Process (Figure 17.3).

Some organizations are so mature in their Knowledge and Risk Management approaches that they have developed a

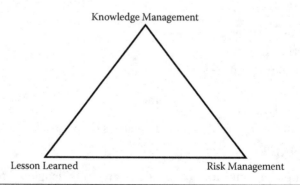

Figure 17.3   Lessons learned relationship.

KBR—Knowledge-Based Risk approach. One of the NASA references summarized their work.

At the NASA Exploratory Systems Mission Directorate (ESMD), Dave Lengyel said "A great way to identify risks is through lessons learned, which in many cases were risks that challenged a previous program. Knowledge-based risk approaches provide that as well as analysis and planning information."

At ESMD, where the future of U.S. human space flight is being shaped, Lengyel believes merging risk and knowledge management is essential, and that it starts with the practitioners. In the ESMD, lessons learned feed the risk management and knowledge management systems. People use information from the knowledge systems to make informed risk assessments.

So, we should be able to state a principle here:

Risk Management should support Knowledge Management and Knowledge Management should support Risk Management. (High maturity, continuous improvement)

Conclusions

What can we conclude from this discussion of the relationship between Risk Management and Knowledge Management and the Data and Information Elements that occupy Knowledge Management space?

1. Organizations that have a robust Project Risk Management Program in place are more likely to have successful project Lessons Learned Processes that can lead to better Data and Information Elements for a Knowledge Management Process.

2. Mature organizations that embrace Knowledge Management and continuous improvement are more likely to have Knowledge Management Processes that are closely linked with Risk Management. Further, the two feed each other to improve all business processes.

3. Artificial Intelligence (also known as Augmented Intelligence in some circles) (AI) is an emerging discipline that has been described as a knowledge management system that thinks. More and more industries will leverage AI in the future to add new dimension to the customer experience and to project

management capabilities to create enhanced outcomes and results for all stakeholders. Lessons learned based on feedback and expanded project requirements will be a way of life that can benefit each of us in our daily lives.

If implemented properly, project Lessons Learned can be a key integrator process that brings Knowledge Management and Risk Management closer together.

18

USING THE PROJECT FRAMEWORK TO FACILITATE TECHNOLOGY DEVELOPMENT IN PROJECTS

Historically, technology has enabled the advancement of civilization by the application of science and engineering to the solution of problems and the needs of society. In addition, technology has fostered "innovation" in developing new products, services, and processes for modern life.

In projects, new technology development has become an integral part of projects turning "strategy" into "action" for both individuals and organizations. The facilitation of new technology development in project organizations has been enabled by the practices and procedures of the Program Management Office (PMO) and the focus on stakeholders as key components of the business and technology requirements process. The PMO is a defined capability. In the future, project managers will utilize both "best practices" and "benchmarking" in their quest for new technologies that will add functionality to their projects and ensure that rapidly changing project business requirements can be met within the schedules, cost, and quality demands of their projects.

Because of rapidly changing entrepreneurial and innovative motivations of new technology application developers, project managers will be challenged to survey the field of new apps daily to see if their projects could benefit from these new and emerging apps.

"Lessons learned" feedback from these efforts and the new project framework can be used to improve new technology development and application in project management.

An "Innovation PMO" Approach to Technology Development

It has been difficult to pick up any literature on business strategy and business growth recently without seeing the word "innovation" splattered all over the headlines and content. Innovation is such a catchy word these days because the idea inspires people; it connotes taking the innovator to a new height of success. Likewise, there are some companies whose names seem to "drip" with the word Innovation whenever you encounter the company's name: DuPont, Procter & Gamble, and Apple, for instance.

A.G. Lafley, in his book *Game Changer: How You Can Drive Revenue and Profit Growth with Innovation,* defines Innovation as "the process of converting or turning new ideas into revenue and profit." ("Value" is another term for this end product.) Similarly, many authors in the PMO field have defined the PMO as a distinct organizational structure that can be used to drive innovation through project management, technology development, and product development. In this sense, the "innovation PMO" is a designed and drafted capability system.

Every year *Strategy + Business* magazine publishes its "Global Innovation 1000" list of the top innovation companies. A recent article titled "The Global Innovation 1000: How the Top Innovators Keep Winning," was based on an ongoing Booz & Company study of innovation of the most successful companies in the innovation game today. Their premise was that "innovation capabilities enable companies to perform specific functions at all the stages of the R&D value chain." The consultants asked the respondents in the Global Innovation 1000 survey which capabilities were most important in achieving and sustaining success in innovation.

Surprisingly, the study found that "all the successful companies surveyed depended on a *common set of critical innovation capabilities.* These include the ability to gain insight into customer needs and to understand the potential relevance of emerging technologies at the ideation stage, to engage actively with customers to prove the validity of concepts during product development, and to work with pilot users to roll out products carefully during commercialization." The study's authors also found important ongoing assessment of market potential during the project selection phase.

You will recall that, in other sections of this book, I have discussed the rise of PMOs for specific purposes in organizations, which recognizes the special value added by having an organization focused on project management capabilities as a means of converting strategy into action. For example, some utilities have formed Smart Grid PMOs to handle Smart Grid projects. In an organization that is determined to succeed and grow in its industry, with best-in-class products, services, or both, why not consider creating an entity called the Innovation PMO? What would the characteristics of such an entity be?

First, since feedback and research from consumers, users, and other stakeholders is critical to understanding "what to innovate for," the Innovation PMO would establish its own unique source of feedback research within the context of its own industry or consumer setting. This is a key element of success. Unfortunately, very few PMOs are currently doing a good job in this area, but to become an Innovation PMO, they must.

Second, the Innovation PMO has leveraged its key supplier and vendor relationships. It knows that, frequently, the unsolicited feedback provided by suppliers and vendors provides a fresh look as to where the market is headed, especially in innovation scenarios.

Closer relationships with suppliers have also resulted in some acquisitions of smaller technology oriented companies to "jump start" the introduction of new technology. For example, in 2016, WalMart acquired a small e-commerce company, Jet.com, to improve its online customer interface and boost online sales of products and services.

Another example is the large number of collaborations between innovation companies and IBM, which utilize WATSON as an accelerator of its technology processes. Large pharmaceutical companies have enhanced their drug development through use of WATSON's abilities to handle large amounts of data, and perform high-speed computations that focus on the combinations of proteins and other compounds in new drugs.

Third, the Innovation PMO has tailored the critical innovation capabilities discussed in the Booz & Company study to the internal business context of the organization. This tailoring process is analogous to the benchmarking process that is used by leading PMO organizations, such as American Express and Procter & Gamble, to establish best practices. Like best practices, to be successful, innovation capabilities can't be lifted verbatim without being tailored to the organization's business context.

In the future, PMOs will design their project management processes to incorporate new technology development as a routine activity. Project managers will require competency in the key technology development skills in recognizing and integrating new apps and technology modifications "on the fly."

Innovation is certain to be a topic embraced by more and more organizations looking for successful growth-promoting projects in their industries. Your role as a PMO practitioner is to find a spot where you can contribute to that success. In this regard, the old expression "Change Creates Opportunity" is a harbinger of success if you embrace new technology development with all of its potential.

A more recent Global Innovation Study from 2016, which is highlighted in the 2017 book *Strategy That Works*, showed that the truly innovative companies today are leveraging cross-functional capabilities to achieve a competitive advantage. The implication for PMOs today and in the future is that they need to look for those areas of technology expertise in the company that will closely match their needs for new technology developments in upcoming projects and develop cross-functional relationships with those areas to bring the expertise to bear when new projects demand new technologies for implementation (Figure 18.1).

The take away for the reader is that PMOs in the future must build "technology development capability systems" to succeed at new projects, which demand new technology. By definition, from the book cited earlier, a "capability system" is the combination of people, processes, technology, and organization that allows an individual or

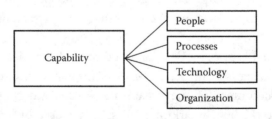

Figure 18.1 The basic components of organizational or individual capability.

organization to deliver its intended outcomes. The blueprint covers all of those components, but not separately. It determines how they will fit together. There is also an accompanying plan that specifies people who will build pieces of the capability, the targets and incentives that will govern their actions, and a timetable for implementation.

Therefore, within the PMO, it is possible to define a "technology development capability system" that focuses on the skills and processes needed in that organization to advance technology development for projects. Their process for building new capability focuses on answering the following questions:

1. What is the capability?
2. Why is it valuable?
3. How would it be different from what we have today?
4. Describe a day-in-the-life of this capability; what does it look like?
5. What is required to make it work?
6. For the "capabilities system," what does the business case look like?
7. How does this capability fit with others in the capability system?

The focus on this analysis was to build meaningful and lasting capabilities and to foster cross-functional relationships between corporate competencies that complement each other. In short, their theme was "build capabilities before seeking results."

To summarize, PMOs in the future will need to develop new technology capabilities systems that will add to their project delivery capabilities. Of course, specialized PMOs in companies such as biopharmaceuticals or information systems will need to consider industry-specific technologies to ensure their "table-stakes" status. This new reality may require a "maturity curve" approach in implementation to be successful in the long term.

With the increasing focus by organizations that projects have a strategic role to create change in organization and their operations, more emphasis is being placed on the Organizational Project Management Maturity Model ("OPM3") so that projects create repeatable and consistent results. The methodology employed by Organizational Project Management Maturity Model is usually an assessment of the current maturity state of the project organizations, such as PMOs, and then a process improvement program that focuses on increasing the organizational maturity.

The new project framework presented in this book for capturing, documenting, and sharing lessons learned can be used to assess the new technology capability as time goes on, and contribute to updates, as needed.

Building capability must also consider building competency of project managers and other PMO staff. Rich Maltzman and Loredano Abraa Abramo provide a good summary of PM competency in their new book *Bridging the PM Competency Gap*.

Focus on Stakeholder Needs for Technology Development Efforts

Because technology can change so rapidly during project planning and execution, it is important for project managers to keep current with stakeholder needs and "final" business requirements of projects.

I would like to propose that we take a new approach to project business and technology requirements definition based on principles of "design thinking." Design Thinking is an approach to innovation. In fact, it has often been called "human-centered innovation" because of the focus on physical, emotional, social, and cognitive needs of the stakeholder or client.

Design thinking has been used successfully by consumer and industrial product companies as well as service providers to open up new markets, define new products, identify new partnerships, and to solidify relationship management for parties involved. Design thinking starts with "empathy," which means looking at things from the viewpoint of the stakeholder, user, or sponsor (Figure 18.2).

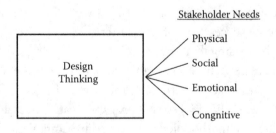

Figure 18.2 Design thinking focus.

Tim Brown, the CEO of IDEO, has written extensively about Design Thinking and his reference book on the subject is *Change by Design*. Also, A.G. Lafley and Ram Charan have written about Design Thinking and its associated facilitating framework known as "integrative thinking" in their book *Game Changer: How You Can Drive Revenue and Profit Growth with Innovation*.

In a *Wall Street Journal* article early in 2010, Estee Lauder CEO Fabrizio Freda, formerly an executive with Procter & Gamble and a leading advocate of Design Thinking in product development at P&G, said "we don't want to just do the products that consumers want. We want to be inspired by consumer desires and surprise them with products that they don't expect." That takes a deep understanding of the cognitive, social, physical, and emotional needs of the clients, consumers, and customers. But it also applies to project business requirements development.

Here are some specific actionable things you can do from a Design Thinking perspective to enhance your business and technology requirements definition:

1. Listen. Employ "empathic communication" to understand the viewpoints of the stakeholders, users, and sponsors. Listen to the "stories" and "anecdotes" that your stakeholders tell each other. Often they will reveal their anxieties, worries, and fears along with other needs that are never mentioned in their straightforward conversations. Engage them in "storytelling." We have discussed the example of the SAP project manager who spoke with everyone who would potentially be affected by the changes introduced by his SAP program. His Empathic Communication elicited many business requirements and business opportunities of a detailed nature. It also built "commitment" from the ground up for the program scope, issues, and approach which the project manager wanted to pursue.

2. Look for analogous situations or scenarios to develop deeper insights into the needs of the customers. Tim Brown, CEO of IDEO, one of the pioneering companies in Design Thinking" techniques often talks about some work they did in redesigning the processes for a hospital emergency room. They talked to so many emergency room "experts" about what could be

done that they decided to seek an analogous situation. So they studied National Association for Stock Car Auto Racing (NASCAR) pit crews. Notice the similarities: high pressure, high competency requirements, and ability to work as a team and as individuals in a time-constrained, close-quarters environment. Often, sharing the analogous scenario with your stakeholders can stir their innovative and creative instincts. I mentioned in a previous post the analogy between project manager and movie director. Look at the similarities between developing movie script, background, character, and actor development and managing a project's requirements.

3. Prototype the business requirements situation as best you can. This will provide additional insights into "real needs."

4. Expand your questioning of stakeholders to other than just "superusers" of the systems or new processes. Tim Brown often tells the story of redesigning cooking utensils for the kitchen. After continually using experienced cooks for requirements gathering, they brought in a group of children and asked them to put the utensils through their paces in some cooking classes. The dexterity and handling requirements were immediately accentuated because the children had very few preconceived ideas about how the utensils were to be used.

5. Read or view some background information on Design Thinking and Integrative Thinking. Lectures by Tim Brown of IDEO can be easily found on the internet. Also, some business school curricula are now embracing Design Thinking as a basic tool for business strategy and requirements gathering. See the work of Heather Fraser at DesignWorks, which is the model school for design thinking at the Rotman School of Management at the University of Toronto. Dean Roger Martin's work on Integrative Thinking can be found in his book *The Opposable Mind*.

This is just the starting point for opening up a whole new panorama of business and technology requirements gathering techniques and validation. Design Thinkers use the whole world experience in their designs. Project managers should do the same using the project framework from this book (Figure 18.3).

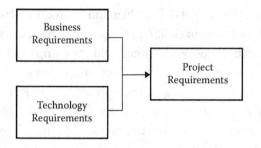

Figure 18.3 Project requirements.

Technology Development—Capturing, Documenting, and Sharing Lessons Learned

In other sections of this book, we have discussed capturing, documenting, and sharing lessons learned from projects using "feedback" from actual project performance information. In today's fast-moving project world, many PMOs use software-based project managements to initiate, plan, execute, and close out their projects. These packages include templates for such tasks as creating project charters, creating and managing project schedules, documenting project review, creating and executing test plans, audit functions, and capturing lessons learned.

In a continuous process improvement framework, these lessons learned would be used to make improvements to the project process so that outcomes from the project would more closely match the intended objectives.

There is much discussion in PMOs today about the best times in the project management cycle to document lessons learned if they are significant to the project objectives. Traditionally, lessons learned have been captured at the project Closeout or during the Final Project Review at the completion of a project. But, with the advent of new digital technology applications, any appropriate time in the project cycle could be designated as a lessons learned capture event. The advantage, of course, in capturing lessons learned more frequently is that improvements to the project process can be made immediately.

Technology Development—Monitoring Risk throughout a Project

Technology development is playing a pivotal role in project management as new technologies impact the decision-making process of project teams to improve functionality of deliverables and to produce new products for the market. Innovation in design processes, materials, electronics, communications, and almost every other field have impacted the approach project teams have taken toward product and project development.

However, new technology development in project and product development also introduces new risks that must be planned for to achieve the outcomes desired by the projects. Many things can happen during new technology development that warrant close monitoring and increased awareness on the part of project teams. New technology development has resulted in many false starts to projects and in replanning and rework during the project.

There are aspects of Risk Management that can be applied during the development stages of projects by the project group or PMO and the vendor proposing the new technology.

Focusing on risk in this manner allows the vendor and the PMO to identify what can be termed controllable and uncontrollable risk. Controllable risks are those components in which the vendor has specialized expertise or previous experience. Uncontrollable risks represent unforeseen risks in the development. This further detailed look enables the vendor and the PMO to lessen the total risk of the new technology development so that the PMO can be reasonably assured that the development would be successful.

An example of the application of these principles is given in the "Case Study—Project Lessons Learned Scenario Technology Development".

Technology Development Project—Project Lessons Learned Summary

What was the Expected Result?	1. Examine project plans, assumptions, deliverables, risk management plans, business case, and financial case for the specific events.
1. Project would be completed on time.	
2. Project would be completed on budget.	
3. All functionality of new system/application would be provided.	
4. New technology development would prove out.	
What was the Actual Result?	1. Analyze actual performance versus expected performance for significant events.
1. Project was completed on time.	
2. Project exceeded budget by $2 million.	
3. With appropriate monitoring, new technology development "proved out."	2. See chapter on selection of "candidates for Lessons Learned."
4. Functionality requirements were met.	

(Continued)

(*Continued*)

What is the Gap? 1. Risk monitoring activity contributed to $2 million over budget condition at close. 2. Risk monitoring probably exceeded usual project risk monitoring activity.	1. For each significant event, define the gap between expected and actual in as much detail as you can.
What is the Lesson to be Learned? 1. In a project which has major technology development but which offers "upside" risk and Benefits Realization at levels of this project, additional Risk Monitoring activity is justified and encouraged. 2. Documentation of Risk Monitoring activity will be included in MS SharePoint and Intranet. 3. An upcoming Project Manager Forum will address the Lessons Learned from this project.	1. For each significant event, summarize in detail the lessons to be learned. 2. Cite risk, new technology prove out, and other key factors.
Comments This project was a good development project for the project manager who is transitioning to a program manager position for his next career move.	

Risk Management Exercises

1. For your project group, write down as many project risks that you have seen for various projects as you can?
2. Discuss with others in your group risks that they have seen in projects.
3. For a specific and significant project risk you have experienced in a project, define a Risk Mitigation Plan with a procedure, any standards and Triggers.

Case Study: Defining Project Requirements for a Lessons Learned Documentation App

You are a project manager working in a PMO that wants to update its ability to capture and document project lessons learned from projects at the end of each major phase of the project. Your task in this case study is to develop the project requirements including business and technology requirements for this project.

Questions:

1. Who are the stakeholders this project is intended to satisfy?
2. How are you currently capturing project lessons learned?
3. Using principles from Design Thinking, define the technology requirements for the project.
4. Does your PMO currently have a technology development capability within the PMO to meet this project goal or will you have to look cross-functionally or even to third parties for such expertise?

Case Study—Project Lessons Learned
Scenario Technology Development

Background: A PMO completed a project to provide new communications equipment for a major business/functional area of the corporation. The vendor selected for the project developed new technology during the course of the project that would allow major specifications of the end deliverables to more closely match the business requirements of the business/functional group. Both the PMO and the business functional group recognized that there was a major risk in this new technology development.

There was some debate between the PMO and the vendor about the likelihood component of the risk, but both parties agreed that, if the risk was realized, there would be a significant component of the impact.

If the technology development was not successful or successful only on a limited basis, the project would have to be delayed for new business requirements and perhaps a new vendor selection. The resulting time to market might put this business/functional group at a competitive disadvantage versus major competitors who were also believed to be developing cutting-edge technology in this communications area.

Focusing on risk in this manner also allowed the vendor and the PMO to identify what they termed controllable and uncontrollable risk. Controllable risks were those components in which the vendor had specialized expertise or previous experience handling.

Uncontrollable risk represented unforeseen risks in the development. This further detailed look enabled the vendor and the PMO to lessen the total risk of the new technology development so that the PMO was reasonably assured that the development would be successful.

The project team monitored the vendor technology development closely during the project and the vendor encountered only minor problems. Each time this happened, the vendor and the PMO project team would meet to decide on a course of action and the resulting impact on overall project risk. However, the additional time for the meetings to assess risk was not included in the original project cost/ budget estimate. The project exceeded budget by $2 million, but the overall Benefits Realization from the introduction of the new technology was in excess of $20 million.

Project Closeout: The project closeout discussion identified this as a candidate for a project Lesson Learned, not because the budgeted cost exceeded by $2 million but because the Project Team, Steering Committee, and Projects Governance Committees agreed that the actions taken by the Project Team to monitor and control risk were worthy to be shared with other project teams. All facts and perspectives were discussed. Although the risk identified at the start of the project was considered a downside risk because of the impact of the risk if an occurrence, the monitoring actions of the project team and vendor throughout the project gave everyone a new perspective.

19

USING FACILITATION AND REFRAMING TOWARD PROJECT PROCESS IMPROVEMENT

As we have seen in our discussion of actionable Lessons Learned, the project manager must take an active role in identifying Lessons Learned as well as working with his project community to determine Significant Events that can become Candidates for project Lessons Learned. This expanded competence on the part of the project manager means that new capabilities must be developed within the PMO and within project managers to fully realize the potential from project Lessons Learned. The following discussion breaks these capabilities into distinct categories:

Facilitation

To gather the various Perspectives that the project team members may have experienced during the project, the project manager must be a good facilitator. Most project managers are skilled in directing teams in collaboration with team members and stakeholders on projects. However, facilitation requires a new dimension in working with team members and stakeholders who may have different opinions about what was significant in a project. Reconciling some of these positions is extremely important in project Lessons Learned.

There is nothing worse in a project Lessons Learned exercise than reaching the conclusion of the exercise, reviewing the project Lessons Learned, and then having one key team member express his view that he did not see or experience a Significant Event in such a way that it would truly qualify as a Significant Event for project Lessons Learned purposes. His interpretation of the truth for a portion of the project was such that he could not reconcile his position with other team members' positions on a key scenario or point for which a Significant Event has been identified by the project team, which in turn has been converted into a Candidate, and finally into a project Lesson Learned. It is the role of the project manager to ferret out such diverse viewpoints, explore them with the team members or stakeholders, and then to "facilitate" the appropriate use of the framework to reach an actionable Lesson Learned.

Reframing

Project managers must also develop the key skill of reframing, which means putting the scenario details in a form that takes account of the most accurate objectives, culture, processes, and structure in place in the organization at the time the Lessons Learned were developed.

When the 2012 Olympics began in London, everyone had the expectation that Michael Phelps would cruise to victory in all his swimming races because of his past history in racking up medals in competition. When he failed to finish in the top four positions in the first swimming event of the 2012 Olympics, some NBC announcers were eager to say that perhaps he was not ready to compete in the 2012 Olympics, and that his hype for medals might be too much. However, one announcer reframed the conversation when he stated that Phelps had not trained for that particular event because it was not one of his signature events. This new information quieted the original announcers, who had declared that Phelps might not be ready. It added a new perspective to the conversation. This is the essence of reframing.

Of course, Phelps ultimately won four gold medals in the later events.

Leader of Discussion at All Levels on Benefits of Lessons Learned

Project managers must be prepared to lead the discussion, at all levels of the organization, with regard to project Lessons Learned, their benefits to the organization and to customers, and how they are developed and contribute to a continuous improvement environment in the organization.

Process Improvement Leader

Project managers must be prepared to interpret the Lessons Learned from other projects and to be prepared to implement them as process improvements at any point in the project community that they are a part of. This implies that they must develop the skills and competencies to fully understand the actionability characteristics of project Lessons Learned.

Exercises

1. From your experiences in the project community, are there additional capabilities that the project manager must exhibit to fully capitalize on project Lessons Learned?
2. How does your project organization handle the facilitation role of the project manager in documenting project Lessons Learned?

20

AVOIDING TRAPS
WHERE STRUCTURE
INFLUENCES BEHAVIOR

Two principles govern Lessons Learned for multiple projects in a project environment:

1. The structure of the project environment influences project and project team behavior.
2. Project environments are dynamically complex. Project environments may be viewed and described by key elements of organizational dynamics, including vision, mental models, systemic structure, patterns of behavior, and events.

The patterns of behavior and project Lessons Learned from the application of the principles set forth earlier add leverage to your efforts to improve overall project performance within the project environment.

This age-old question "Does structure influence behavior?" is still asked every day by people who understand the answer already, and by those who have never seen it posed before.

What Is Structure?

Structure means the policies, standards, processes, and procedures that set the stage for how the corporation and its individual organizational units carry out business on a daily basis.

For those of you who may have trouble visualizing how structure might influence behavior, let me offer an example from my experience. Many years ago, I worked as a product planner for a major domestic automotive manufacturer in the Detroit area. One of the benefits offered to top executives of the division and the company was a company automobile. Each morning, when the executive arrived at the building, he or she was met by a service technician who asked if the executive had encountered any problems or had any service items that needed attention. At the end of the day, each executive drove away from the facility with a clean, serviced automobile.

With this backdrop, consider the following scenario. At one time, a certain service problem was identified in the field and reported through the service warranty network to the company. Reports and metrics summarizing the problem were reported through the ranks and eventually were highlighted to the executives in charge of product quality. However, none of the executives had personally encountered the problem—or if they had encountered it, the problem was fixed with "same-day service." The personal experiences of executives led them to refuse to believe that the reports accurately identified the extent of the problem in the field. The reported problems were not taken seriously. In some cases, only one executive in 20 might have encountered the problem and, if he or she wasn't assigned to product quality, the problem was forgotten as just another minor flaw. As a result, the division failed to react to a mounting service problem. The structure of the executives' benefits—the company car and daily service—had influenced behavior to such an extent that there was actually denial that a problem existed.

This same structural behavior exists in project environments throughout industry today where the policies, processes, and standards put in place by the organization often influence project team behavior and subsequently project outcomes.

Let's examine another example a little closer to home in the Program Management Office (PMO). In my experience, in the early days of defining new PMO processes and procedures, we recognized the need to define some rules for Project Justification and Approval. These rules called for the project teams to develop a Business Case to justify the project. As in similar situations with other PMOs, we attempted to define some structure to answer the questions: (1) how extensive does the Business Case analysis need to be and (2) who should be reviewing it for final signoff as an approved project? An early attempt to define this standard resulted in a rule that every proposed project over $1 million total cost must have a full Business Case with all economics, and it must be signed off by the IT Authorization Board. All projects under $1 million total cost must define a partial business case with limited economics and must be signed off by a subset of the IT Authorization Board.

Now, what happened? You could probably guess that there were many projects proposed at $900,000, or two projects proposed at $800,000 and $850,000, which could easily have been combined into a more strategic and doable project. Remember: Structure influences behavior. Well-meant or intended actions can often lead to unintended consequences.

As I stated earlier, the potential exists for far-reaching leveraging actions to be taken regarding the project environment and the structure of that environment, which could benefit all future projects and provide meaningful insights into project team behavior. And the resulting implications for Knowledge Management are just as great. Knowledge focused on the project environment can provide insights into how we design future project communities that are robust, productive, team inspiring, and which lead to greater success for all projects.

This was the subject of my paper presentation at the Third Knowledge and Project Management Symposium in Tulsa in August 2008. The systemic thinking and organizational dynamics principles of Peter Senge and Daniel Kim as outlined later involves viewing the world at various levels of depth, from the most obvious level of day-to-day events, to the patterns of behavior that can often be discerned by studying organizational groups, to the systemic structure that is often in place as a result of the mental models and vision that people exhibit in an organizational setting (Figure 20.1).

Often the vision may be shared (or unshared) and the mental models may only exist in the minds of the people making up the organization or group. However, these mental models may be so strong that they contribute to recurring behavior in the form of systemic structure (Table 20.1).

Systemic structure often leads to patterns of behavior, which are manifest in the behaviors of individuals and teams (including project teams) to support the underlying structure in place.

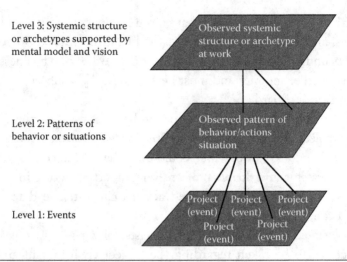

Level 3: Systemic structure or archetypes supported by mental model and vision

Observed systemic structure or archetype at work

Level 2: Patterns of behavior or situations

Observed pattern of behavior/actions situation

Level 1: Events

Project (event) Project (event) Project (event) Project (event) Project (event)

Figure 20.1 Organizational dynamics levels of thinking.

Using these principles from Peter Senge and Daniel Kim, I looked at several projects in a corporate environment that were playing in the same space.

In other words, they were subject to the same project environmental structure, policies, and procedures. The project team behavior in each case was driven by that structure or by the policies in place. So the leveraging factor in improving the performance of those project teams and the projects resided in an examination of the project environment.

On the basis of my experience as a project manager, project coordinator, and internal consultant in several PMOs, I have developed some observations about project Lessons Learned from both the individual projects and the project environment that provide some insights into how we can move forward to structure Knowledge Management systems that best capture and leverage the lessons for future project community.

Let's look at several examples from a PMO project situation.

First, let's examine the scenario in which a PMO expressed an interest in using local (meaning geographic) resources for final implementation of a worldwide project to save costs for the project. The project plan is stated as such. However, the project manager did not communicate this plan well to the local management of the local resources to be used, and the local resources were not always available during the implementation phase of the project. This same pattern of activity was

Table 20.1   Systems Thinking and Organizational Dynamics Framework

LEVEL OF REASONING	TOPIC	DESCRIPTION
High leverage and high complexity	Vision	All of these levels are informed by vision. The key question at this level is "What do we want to create?" or "What do we seem to be creating?" These aspirations, stated or unstated, exert a powerful influence on the events, patterns of behavior, systemic structures, and mental models working in any given situation.
	Mental models	Systemic structures are frequently held in place by the assumptions or mental models. These assumptions maybe theories on what constitutes quality, good service, or an acceptable return on investment. These theories in use may also treat interpersonal dynamics; for example, approaches toward conflict or the correct way to interact with senior leaders. They may also be implied in project actions: "Our key project drivers are schedule and cost."
	Systemic structure	Once a pattern has been identified and described, it is possible to document the systemic dynamics that maintain it. The level of systemic structures marks the boundary between what can be easily be observed in the objective world (events and patterns) and what must be assessed from the data (mental models and vision). Systemic dynamics are abstractions but they stay close to the data.
	Patterns of behavior	The causal loop language described in *The Fifth Discipline* by Peter Senge is an example of this kind of thinking. Systems archetypes have been identified for recurring patterns of behavior in organizations. The most significant for an organization just becoming aware of systems thinking are limits to growth and underinvestment.
Low leverage and low complexity	Events	There is nothing wrong with understanding the world as a series of events. It is just not a leveraged way to approach problems. Leverage begins with pattern recognition, with the basic insight that this has happened before. Most discussions begin at the events level with some version of "this is what happened." Discussions at this level usually assign a single cause to each effect. "This happened because that happened." Listen to an explanation of stock market behavior on any given day for a good example of reasoning at the event level. In project terms, the events are individual projects, and the cause and effect are the project Lessons Learned.

identified for several other projects that planned to use local resources to control budgeted costs but did not communicate well with local management. Because there was no record of Lessons Learned identifying this deviation, the pattern continued until an Organizational Change Management consultant uncovered it while planning for a new global project implementation. Structure influences behavior.

In terms of the archetypical structure in place, this behavior resembled a tragedy of the commons situation, in which local resources were always being identified for use in implementations without regard for the number of resources or their actual availability.

Second, let's examine a situation in which a project involved certain security features and applications that the project manager assumed would be supplied by the Infrastructure Security group by dedication of the appropriate security resources at the appropriate time in the project. This is an example of using part-time resources in lieu of full-time resources in the hope that the part-time resources would be less costly to the project budget because they were technically assigned to a Corporate Infrastructure Group. In actuality, when the implementation phase occurred, a high-priority security crisis always seemed to occur at the same time. The result was delay in project completion and higher incurred costs. This pattern continued until an audit revealed that the pattern was in play. Structure influences behavior.

One of the key factors that contribute to the project environment playing such a role in key Lessons Learned is the dynamic complexity inherent in the project environment. This was first recognized and documented in several Project Management Institute papers in the late 1990s. Dynamic complexity is a condition arising from the number of population factors, variables, and connectivity of the networks that make up modern project life. It is a consequence of the integration of many factors. Most often, dynamic complexity is manifest in projects in which cause and effect are not close in space and time, and therefore, actions or decisions taken on the part of key project participants often manifest themselves in unintended consequences relative to the original actions. Another characteristic of this pattern is that seemingly obvious actions on the part of participants introduce unexpected results.

I would like to give an example of such dynamic complexity, which will pave the way for us addressing the dynamic complexity of the project environment. Several years ago, in a series of newspaper articles, the subject of teen drivers, accidents, and deaths was addressed in a detailed manner. Of course, this was nothing new. Over the past 20–30 years, it had been well documented that there was a high correlation between teen drivers under certain conditions and highway deaths involving the teen drivers as well as their passengers. But the dynamic complexity of this situation did not put light on the issue until more recently. For example, a teen death from driving in Kentucky did not have a great impact on people in Indiana. The cause and effect were not close in space and time. Also, different state jurisdictions regarding teen drivers and driver's licenses were not well coordinated until recent years. If one state took actions that it thought necessary due to statistics gathered within that state, other states were not likely to pay much attention because of their own rules and the wishes of parents and guardians. Often the parents and guardians of teen drivers reacted to teen driver deaths as isolated incidents and not to be taken as a rule-making scenario in their case because of influences that said that every teen should be given driving privileges to ease the burden on parents or guardians.

It was not until some definitive patterns of behavior that cut across state lines and across various stakeholder groups emerged that people and organizations began to take an interest. Insurance studies and Federal Highway Administration studies, coupled with sharing of information among states, led to some very significant observations of patterns of driver behavior:

Teens driving alone in a car or with one or two other teen passengers without a supervising adult in the evening, and especially in rural areas or states which had more lax rules, regulations, and enforcement of laws, were identified as having a high probability of being involved in a fatal accident.

Analyzing the individual accidents as isolated events often led to characterization that high speed or not negotiating a curve were the real causes of the crashes.

The dynamic complexity of this situation was manifest in the number of stakeholders, number of distinct jurisdictional areas, lack of sharing of crucial trend data, and a reluctance on the part of parents and guardians to face up to the true realities of the teen driver incapacity to handle the situations.

Further detail that may be used to develop a more detailed case study around this example may be found in Appendix 3 on dynamic complexity and teen drivers.

Exercises

1. Describe several situations in your own project organization where structure influenced behavior of project personnel or teams.

2. Think of several projects in your project environment and the behaviors, actions, and results of project teams in carrying out those projects. Are there any similarities in project behavior that you can identify and document?

21

LESSONS LEARNED FROM THE APPLICATION OF ORGANIZATIONAL DYNAMICS TO THE BUSINESS CONTINUATION AND EMERGENCY RESPONSE ENVIRONMENT

Introduction

As a generality, Business Continuation and Emergency Response initiatives are conducted as projects, and the practitioners are project managers. These individuals have become an integral part of the "strategic" processes of companies due to the need to respond quickly to emergencies and to have plans in place to restore business operations as quickly as possible in the event of a business disruption for any reason. Because environmental, social, organizational, and behavioral issues are always in a state of flux in modern organizations, Lessons Learned are as important to these project managers as the initial planning process for business continuation.

This chapter presents an organizational and strategic "perspective" on the impact of Organizational Dynamics on the overall performance of organizations that employ Business Continuity (BC) Management (BCM). It employs both organizational dynamics and strategic thinking for BCM in making its conclusions.

BCM has been defined by the British Standards Institute as "a holistic, management process that identifies threats to an organization and the impacts to business operations that the threats, if realized, might cause, and which provides a framework for building organizational resilience with the capability for an effective response that safeguards the interests of its key stakeholders, reputation, brand, and value-creating activities."

BCM is a process with multiple distinct activities or subprocesses.

Business Continuity as a Dynamic Process

BC is a "dynamic" process that reacts to changes in the business, as the business itself reacts to changes in threats to the business posed by natural events, accidents, man-made events, geopolitical moves, and other various threats.

BC must change rapidly to keep abreast of the dynamics of its environment.

A great example of a rapidly changing environment is the recent credit card security breach that occurred at Target stores. As you may remember, Target discovered that a malware program had been installed on their Point-of-Service credit card "swipe" machines, upon which customers swiped their credit cards to pay for their purchases. The breach involved nearly all of Target's nearly 2,000 stores, and likely affected more than a million transactions. The malware stole the personal credit card information of customers and compromised the security of that information and their credit card.

Target ultimately ended up offering one year of free credit monitoring to all customers who shopped at their stores that year—but that remedy was not quickly forthcoming. Rather, after a number of days during which Target's management was not providing enough information to customers about their internal actions to safeguard their customers' credit card information, a Twitter campaign was launched by customers to share their experiences in the security breach.

This Twitter campaign proved to be a dynamic situation by which social media played a vibrant and important role in filling the void for information. Target, for its part, was forced to adapt and react—quickly—not only to news of the massive data breach but also to the public relations pressures placed upon it by the Twitter campaign. BC is not a place for the complacent!

BC is an international topic of interest, especially in emerging markets, where it has played a significant role in assisting organizations to respond rapidly to changing threats.

Business Continuity as a Capability

Business Continuity (BC) is a "capability."

A Capablity is a collection of competencies, processes, frameworks, and systems that an organization has assembled to carry out its goals and objectives, and to add value to the organization in some form.

"Systems," for these purposes, refer to any technology that supports a business function, including, but not limited to, any combination of hardware and software.

For purposes of this discussion, we are assuming that the BCM Process consists of three distinct stages:

1. Development
2. Implementation
3. Maintenance

The various elements of BCM thus sort-in to these three stages in the following manner:

Development

- Program initiation
- Risk assessment
- Business impact analysis (BIA)
- Strategy development

Implementation

- Emergency response plan
- Disaster recovery plan
- Business continuity plan

Maintenance

- Awareness and training
- Testing and exercising
- Maintaining and updating

In the world of BCM, "threats" are ubiquitous and represent possible sources of negative impact to organizations. Threats can be natural, accidental, or man-made, and they can lead to disruptions in operations that can adversely impact an organization.

Significant threats that warrant further consideration are identified during the Risk Assessment aspect of the Development Stage.

BC also relies on the presence, availability, and actions of specialized human resource expertise in the organization in areas such as information technology, security, legal, safety, health, environmental, marketing brand management, social media, communications, etc.

Many of these resources have multiple connotations, and they may reside in different locations in the organization. For example, "Security" may refer to physical security, systems security, personal security, management security, etc.

Throughout this chapter, we will discuss how the location, availability, and responsiveness of these specialized resources contribute to both organizational performance (OP) and to individual and team behaviors.

In the following sections, we will discuss how Capability building and development can lead to behaviors that are both positive and negative in terms of OP.

Capability Development by Organizations— The Case of Project Management

In many organizations, an example of the development of Capabilities to create outcomes and results for an organization can be found in the formation and activity of a Program Management Office (PMO).

As organizations sought to improve their performance in the 1980s and 1990s, they began to shift more of their work from "initiatives" and "operations" to "projects." Projects were seen as the method by which the organization could convert strategy into action in the organization.

As project organizations expanded and became more mature, organizations frequently established a PMO when they sought to develop "repeatability" and "consistency" in their project outcomes and results.

PMOs put methodology and processes into place to guide their project plans and workplans. Often these workplans can be simple, involving only four distinct processes: i.e. initiation, planning, execution, and close.

As organizations monitored the results of these methodologies, feedback from stakeholders, customers, auditors, and clients often forced them to dig a layer deeper in their overall project management process.

A logical next step was to add additional Capabilities—such as Risk Management and Vendor Management, for example—to the methodology and project process. Naturally, these new Capabilities required specialized resources that did not exist in the PMO. Usually, resources from Corporate Risk Management and vendor resources from Purchasing and Procurement were "borrowed" as a first step in making Risk Management and Vendor Management fully functioning Capabilities.

This is exactly the point, however, where organizations became misaligned with their new Capabilities. The PMO sought the efforts of Risk Management and Vendor Management to improve performance, but relied on borrowed resources from other dedicated groups. As we will discuss in greater detail later, a number of systems archetypes come into play when an organization is relying upon borrowed resources, and these archetypes can result in the organization's goals becoming misaligned (and the organization not achieving the wanted results).

Like BC, Project Management and its component Capabilities are dynamic in a number of respects. As we discussed earlier, the effectiveness of BC in any organization is affected by the "structure" existing in the organization. This is the same with Project Management.

The accomplishment of project results in the discipline of Project Management is facilitated—for better or for worse—through structure. Structure refers to those policies, standards, processes, practices, and procedures that an organization puts into place to develop the outcomes and results for the organization. Structure, coupled with management's objectives, creates the force for producing outcomes and results.

But, Capabilities such as Project Management and BC also require specialized expertise and resources.

A good example is Security resources. In project management, if a project requires specialized Security resources, often the PMO borrows those resources from a group such as the Information Technology group, where the Security resources have a dedicated home. On the other hand, if the PMO had been organized from "grass roots," with perfect foresight, it would already contain all the expertise and resources needed; there would be no need for the PMO to be borrowing or securing resources from other dedicated groups.

Thus, in most circumstances, a PMO will be required to borrow resources to achieve the organization's goals. And effective borrowing—and true capability building—requires "collaboration" and "commitment" between and among business groups in the same or similar functions and across organizational lines. This Collaboration and Commitment are keys to achieving the results and outcomes desired by the project organization. Accordingly, much effort is expended by PMO groups and project leadership to foster Collaboration and Commitment.

Moreover, problems can arise where the organization's Capabilities evolve more quickly than the organization's structure. In Capability-focused organizations, such as PMOs, OP is the result of—and highly dependent upon—development, learning, behavior, activity, and process (including process improvement based on Lessons Learned). These steps are similar to those employed in the BC Process.

Business Continuity and Organizational Performance

BC is an international topic of interest, especially in emerging markets, where it has played a significant role in assisting organizations to respond rapidly to changing threats.

In an earlier section, we discussed the perspective that BC is a Capability that has been employed by many organizations to improve the resilience of their business functions. Recent studies have determined that in emerging markets, BC, when employed in an organization, can have a positive impact on Organizational Performance (OP).

Here are some various ways in which BCM improves OP:

- Format: BCM positively impacts OP.
- Effectiveness: BIA helps the organization become more effective.
- Efficiency: BCM allows the organization to understand its resources and deploy them more efficiently.
- Quality: BCM imposes standards (in addition to ISO standards).
- Profitability: BCM improves profitability through the effective implementation of BC and disaster recovery plans.

- Quality of Work Life: The culture of BCM becomes embedded in the organization.
- Innovation: BCM requires cross-disciplinary teams, and the innovative development of various backup, and continuity solutions, strategies, and options.
- Productivity: BCM may improve productivity by improving physical security implementing closed circuit television (CCTV), monitoring access, and employing biometrics.

Organizations that deploy BC can expect improved performance in a number of the metrics mentioned earlier.

Organizational Dynamics—Structure and Behavior

An age-old question that is keenly important to this discussion is: "Does structure influence behavior?" Many studies have shown that the answer is decidedly, "yes."

Since behavior also influences performance, we must also examine the organizational dynamics of Capability-developing organizations. The organizational dynamics framework that we are using here is shown as follows:

The individual activities that take place in an organization are a result of individual and team behavior. But they may—and usually are—influenced by Structure. Often, the activities within an organization can be linked through "patterns of behavior" that are discernible within the organization. Once these "patterns" have been established, you can often identify various systems archetypes at play that show the relationships between activities and resources. These systems archetypes are nourished by the mental models, vision, and management goals and objectives that the organization and its participants are guided by each day.

Another way of depicting how individual activities form patterns of behavior and systems archetypes is shown in Chapter 20 in Figure 20.1.

Typical systems archetypes that have frequently been identified in organizations include the following:

- Limits to growth
- Growth and underinvestment

- Fixes that fail
- Success to the successful
- Tragedy of the Commons
- Accidental adversaries

As their names suggest, these systems archetypes typically are systems that negatively impact the organization.

So, as we began to see earlier in the discussion of Capability Management in PMOs, the structure that creates the capability (in this case, BC) that is being employed to obtain improved outcomes and results, is *also* the structure that influences behaviors in such a way that may result in these detrimental systems archetypes, and detract from OP.

How can we develop our capabilities without being hamstrung by these systems archetypes?

Implications of Capability Building for Performance

As we began to see in our discussion of capability management in PMOs, capability-building organizations are characterized by their use of specialized expertise in human resources and by collaboration between or among business groups. These two characteristics contribute to behavior in teams and among stakeholders that may result in patterns of behavior and systems archetypes.

Two prevalent systems archetypes at work in organizations that develop BC as a capability are the "Tragedy of the Commons" and the "Accidental Adversaries" systems archetypes. Until they are addressed, both of these systems archetypes expend resources while producing only limited results.

Tragedy of the Commons

The "Tragedy of the Commons" is an archetype that may be familiar while studying economic history. The archetype derives its name from a scenario that took place in Old England, where individuals or groups would assemble their sheep herds around a grassy area, known as the "Commons," that was owned in common by the townspeople, and which could be used by everyone in that town.

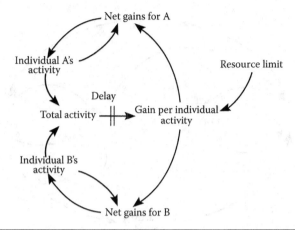

Figure 21.1   Systems archetype "Tragedy of the Commons".

As one might imagine, since no one individual took responsibility for the health of the land, everyone grazed their sheep on the land indiscriminately—even when it led to the land becoming overgrazed and barren, and not available for anyone's use.

This systems archetype is depicted in Figure 21.1.

The "Tragedy of the Commons" systems archetype may be at work whenever there are scarce or specialized resources (i.e., "the Commons") being employed by an organization to accomplish its goals and objectives. Resource usage, depletion, or availability of resources at critical points in a program may become issues.

This is particularly the case in the BC process because specialized expertise and resources are often called upon to react to identified Threats. Typically, these specialized resources reside in parts of the organization that are not under the direct control of BCM. Rather, BC initiatives typically employ Service Level Agreements or project resource assignments to obtain these specialized resources.

Accidental Adversaries

The Accidental Adversaries systems archetype may be observed when two organizations or groups that seemingly would benefit from working closely together instead seek to maximize their own group's goals without optimizing the goals of working together. This is depicted in Figure 21.2.

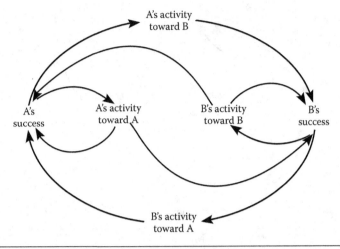

Figure 21.2 Systems archetypes "Accidental Adversaries".

The Accidental Adversaries systems archetype often arises in BC organizations when two organizational groups have different levels of commitment to the BC objectives of the organization, or when an internal business function must work with an external agency such as an Emergency Response or Crisis Management group or a regulatory group.

The impact of these archetypes on OP is profound. It leads to redoing work, redesigning projects, a lack of available resources at critical times, or depletion of critical resources. This means that there is a lengthening of time needed to create results, and that there must be a more collaborative effort among groups to accomplish meaningful results. These effects can be found among all the elements of performance measures mentioned in a previous section of this book. These two archetypes—Tragedy of the Commons and Accidental Adversaries—have consistently been identified as challenges faced by capability-building organizations.

The roles of mental models, and of management goals and objectives, also cannot be overemphasized in this framework. If an organization's Management creates a "tone" and "culture" that emphasizes "cost control," "resource control," or "schedule control," then Management will promote initiatives and projects that emphasize using resources from other groups that are not dedicated to the effort, or collaborative arrangements that ultimately thwart true commitment to the overall

BC or Project Management tasks at hand. As we have seen, these scenarios can often promote behaviors that adversely affect OP.

Recommendations for Business Continuity Management

Every organization is perfectly aligned and/or designed to get the results it gets.

This means that the business processes and the systems that support them are aligned and/or designed to either give optimal performance or less than optimal performance. As we have seen throughout this chapter, for example, whenever human resources are dedicated to a function, alignment is more likely to occur. If resources must be acquired from other groups, however, alignment is hindered.

As BC evolves as a Capability, Management must be more aware of the impact of misalignment between the BC process, and the systems and resources that support it. More misalignment leads to more dysfunction.

When are these behaviors, patterns, and systems archetypes most likely to detract from your organization's total OP?

1. During merger and acquisition activity

   During merger/acquisition activity, groups are being formed and disbanded continuously. Management objectives may (or may not) foster the commitment of individuals to contribute to the overall good of the organization.

2. During Capability-building periods

   As capabilities are expanded or modified in an organization, collaboration and information sources may change noticeably.

3. During highly dynamic business activity and changes in markets

   The dynamic nature of business functions within changing markets can exert influence on BC as a capability to expand its focus.

4. During major changes in threats

   New and more sophisticated threats are becoming the norm for BC. As these threats change, the organization must react and often does so through unintended behaviors.

Conclusions

BC, when employed to improve resiliency of an organization, can improve OP. However, management must be careful to appreciate the "dynamics" of the BC environment, and the impact that the availability of expertise and resources can have on behavior and ultimately on OP.

It is likely that, as BC expands its capability umbrella for an organization, more dedicated and highly skilled resources will be required to support BCM. Organizations must be willing and able to supply these resources.

Also, the issues of collaboration and commitment among groups will continue to be a source of behavior in BCM organizations that may produce unintended consequences.

These issues represent opportunities for managements to fully realize the contribution of BCM to the strategic focus and viability of the modern organization.

The lessons learned for management from this analysis is that, whenever a discipline like BC requires specialized resources from several organizational groups, these resources may become "depleted" in the normal course of operations. In the case where new capabilities require close collaborations among many groups for success, "Accidental Adversaries is a possible outcome of the collaborations because of management structure of the operations.

This has a special significance for project managers and PMO practitioners who aspire to be PMO management because they need to understand not only lessons learned from project performance as covered in earlier parts of the book but also how to establish processes, standards, and policies which lead to desired behaviors on the part of the PMO.

22
THE SUSTAINABILITY IMPERATIVE

When I was an undergraduate student in the late 1960s at the Georgia Institute of Technology in Atlanta (popularly known as Georgia Tech), the president of the institute announced a bold initiative to create a visionary plan for 1985. The plan would define what the institute would "look like." The plan would not only be a "point-in-time" snapshot plan for 1985, but inevitably it would also be a "transition" plan for the interim years.

My classmates joined me in thinking what a bold objective the plan would satisfy, but we really did not pay much attention. We graduated, joined the military and/or graduate school, and started families and careers. Many of us contributed to selected aspects of the plan as it proceeded toward 1985.

In 1985, the Institute President reviewed the results with all alumni and friends and detailed the many diverse areas that it touched. The plan detailed how the boundaries of the Atlanta campus had expanded from its 1960s location in the northwest corner of North Avenue and the I75/I85 corridor in downtown Atlanta, to north of the Tenth Street boundary and east of the I75/I85 corridor. It told of the resources, human physical, emerging digital, intellectual, and investment resources, which were required to achieve the plan. It told of the expansion of academic disciplines into areas such as biomedical engineering, advanced materials, electrical and computer engineering, and systems/control engineering, all of which were now mainstays of Tech's academic and research environment. It told of the collaborations and joint efforts that Tech had undertaken with other universities such as Emory University in Atlanta, Loughborough University in the UK, and several Asian universities. It detailed the many close associations with organizations such as NASA, Coca-Cola, AT&T, Exxon, General Electric, American Express, P&G,

etc. It detailed the relationship with the City of Atlanta, and the establishment of several satellite campuses. The plan also summarized the growing role of the Advanced Technology Development Center as an incubator for new entrepreneurial businesses based on new technology development.

Obviously, any organization such as Georgia Tech that has evolved and grown since 1885, has many degrees of freedom and attachments to a myriad of interests. All of these are important to its future as a technology-focused academic and research institution.

As I recently reflected on this 1985 plan, and my initial reaction to its inception announcement from the late 1960s, it seemed to me that this scenario was really a "metaphor" for "sustainability plan efforts" today. Not only did the plan address the point-in-time snapshot of Georgia Tech in 1985, it also addressed the "transition" to 1985 with considerations for all the impacts to "stakeholders," resource utilization, intellectual issues, energy, organizational issues, etc. In other words, *the subject of sustainability is human interactions in all its forms.*

Sustainability is often described as a quality or condition of a state or process that seeks to strike a balance between the needs and resource utilization of current populations, and those of future populations.

The concern for how current resources are being used, plus the concern for how future resources may be impacted by current actions, is the essence of "sustainability."

In engineering school, we employed a "control volume" to isolate a "system" and detail the inflows and outflows from the "control volume." The basis for this approach was, of course, conservation of mass and energy. Any inflow or outflow of materials and resources across the boundaries of the Control Volume had to be accounted for, no matter how they arose. A chemical reaction within the system, for example, could create energy and material that might flow outside the Control Volume. This is a great depiction for how "sustainability" might operate (Figure 22.1).

But the real message from this scenario is that we all must care about "sustainability," because we all are tied together by interactions and collaborations and relationships that mean that every action is felt by everyone else. No action is taken in a vacuum without some impact to others.

Sustainability is a diverse topic that will require goal setting for the future by anyone or any organization that currently uses or plans to

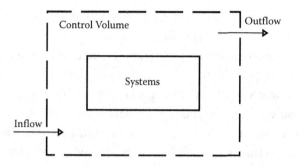

Figure 22.1   Control volume scenario.

use scarce resources in the conduct of day-to-day life. We mentioned this in Chapter 1 because Process and Project have sustainability implications.

Sustainability has many "faces" in today's modern world and in the complexity of the entire human existence. As world population continues to increase, the awareness of all the contributions to and components of sustainability become increasingly important to all humans and living creatures on earth.

Scholar and author Jeffrey Sachs, in his book *The Age of Sustainable Development,* has called for the establishment of "sustainability goals" for the future to guide humans and the world in a direction that will assure a place and resources for future generations. Readers are encouraged to use the process techniques for building sustainability into projects, which can be found in the book *Green Project Management* by Rich Maltzman and David Shirley.

Sustainability not only involves "resources" planned and utilized in projects and processes in everyday life. At least three other topics have been covered in this book that affect sustainability: energy, win–win, and structure.

Resources

This book has introduced a framework for capturing, documenting, and sharing project Lessons Learned using the "feedback" from actual performance information from the project itself. This framework can form the basis for a continuous process improvement framework. This project framework can contribute positively to a sustainable environment where resource utilization in projects is continually monitored for amount and skill level required.

Processes from different organizations can often come into conflict if they are competing for highly skilled or valuable resources that are controlled or owned by a third party. As we have discussed, when these resources are demanded by several organizations, a condition called "Tragedy of the Commons" can result, in which the resources are spread too thin, or are depleted, and do not add value to any of the competing organizations.

Process improvement scenarios can often result in "resource" changes that might impact sustainability.

Energy and Effort

Energy and/or effort is expended when individuals or organizations design, define, or modify processes through process improvement initiatives.

Process improvement requires attention and effort to make it successful.

Win–Win

In an earlier chapter, we discussed "integrative thinking," an approach to project planning and execution which seeks to gain "win–win" solutions to projects rather than compromise solutions that leave some parties in the project outcomes with less than an optimal position.

Win–win solutions support the goals and objectives and the internal workings of the organizations involved in the projects. Effort and commitment is maximized in such organizations. This sets the stage for future project work that is satisfying and can contribute positively to the organization and its goals.

Win–win, when combined with process improvement methods, can result in the growth of organizations.

Structure

By definition, "Structure" is policies, standards, procedures, practices, and processes that have been put in place by an organization that may influence the behavior of individuals in the organization. When Structure meets some management objectives for the way processes or projects are managed, the possibility of unintended consequences may become a reality.

We have given examples of some of these scenarios in other chapters in the book. A good recent example of this is the Wells Fargo program in the southwestern states of Arizona and California, in which corporate compensation incentives for promoting and selling certain bank "products" led to local management, in its attempts to gain the corporate compensation incentives, promoting the credit cards to unsuspecting customers, some of whom management required that they obtain credit cards to meet certain goals. In addition, many of these customers were not qualified by credit terms to have the cards, which resulted in an unintended consequence situation. Wells Fargo corporate management has recently taken action with regard to this situation with its local managements.

In this case, a process was put in place, which interacted with a management goal to produce the unintended consequence. Sustainability implications include an increased amount of management attention to Structure and its consequences.

In terms of sustainability, management should, at planned intervals, examine their Structure to determine whether the outcomes match intentions. Process improvement methods discussed in this book can be helpful in aligning Structure with outcomes. A number of project examples have been given in this book.

Conclusion

Sustainability is directly related to the major topics in this book: Process, Project, Research, Capability, Lessons Learned, Risk Management, Knowledge Management, Process Improvement, etc. Resource utilization, energy and effort, structural implications, and approaches to projects that create Win–Win solutions are all subjects in this book.

Sustainability is no longer a nice-to-have feature. It is an imperative in all facets of modern life.

23
Conclusions

Obviously, project Lessons Learned come from postproject completion analysis. Project Lessons Learned are intended to inform and
impact the future behavior of new and existing project managers in new future projects, where similar project environments were
considered the "as is" process state. By using some systemic thinking
principles, it is possible to affect the behavior and results of many
projects playing in the same space by making changes in the project
environment. This is often termed as leveraging actions to the project
portfolio.

Now what does that really mean?

The project environment is composed of the external corporate environment and the internally created corporate environment.
Usually, the organizational and governance structures for a Program
Management Office (PMO) group are defined and evolve over time
as the organization evolves. The structure put in place by the organization has a great deal to do with how people act, behave, and make
decisions within that project environment.

We have already introduced the expression that structure
influences behavior. The structure of the project environment is
made up of policies, standards, procedures, defined relationships,
reporting linkages, etc., that constitute the working environment
within the firm. We are also aware that, in the dynamic complexity
of project environments these days, well-intended actions can lead
to unintended consequences. John Sterman at MIT has studied this
type of behavior extensively. This is because the cause and effect are
not close in space and time, and some nonlinearity may occur in
which an action or decision on the part of a person or group may lead
to unintended actions or behavior by others based on their interpretations in their business context. John Sterman has stated that,
"the goal of systems thinking and systems dynamics modeling is to

improve our understanding of the ways in which an organization's performance is related to its internal structure and operating policies, including those of customers, competitors, and suppliers, and then to use that understanding to design high-leverage policies for success."

Organizations and groups have the ability to anticipate and plan what effects their PMO structures will have on project behaviors. Accordingly, they can take actions over time to react and adapt to unintended results that are occurring as a result of the structure of the project environment. The project environment is a dynamic phenomenon—we can adjust structure in order to influence project behavior. This approach to project management, however, is just in its infancy and requires some art along with the science.

So, the bottom line for those of you who are designing new PMOs, or who are working with existing PMOs that have a set of policies, standards, and procedures in place to guide the planning and execution of projects is this—follow some simple evaluation points I present here to lessen the risk that you will introduce some unintended consequences from your project environment:

1. Develop some scenarios to test out your policies, standards, processes, and procedures. Take a typical project and follow it through the Project Management Process to see what the behavior of project managers, team members, sponsors, or other stakeholders might be.

2. If your policies and processes have been in place for some length of time, test them to see if the thresholds for governance committee reviews are still valid. In other words, over time, your PMO projects may have taken on different characteristics that have increased costs. The threshold values for review and signoff may no longer adequately cover the portfolio as you had originally planned.

3. If new technology is introduced rapidly into your process, have a review process in place to determine *at the earliest point possible* in the process if the new technologies are compatible with current technologies and infrastructure. Otherwise, you will likely incur additional costs for these new technologies when they are evaluated.

4. Check the hurdle rates for your economic/financial analysis in your business cases at intervals to ensure that they are set consistently with the business objectives and the types of projects that you are deploying.

5. Survey your Project Authorization Governance Groups occasionally to make sure there is consistency in the way each member of the group is viewing the mission and value proposition that projects present to the organization.

6. Examine key reporting relationships for the project team within the PMO and understand how the overall structure of the PMO influences where decisions are made and who makes them.

7. Identify and monitor any cultural or business context issues that might play a major role in the project environment for your organization or industry. Since these variables are dynamic and change over time, make sure you are evaluating all projects on a consistent basis. This is, of course, easier said than done. It involves being a student of the project environment and touching base with others in the PMO to ensure all bases are covered.

8. Continue to look at project Lessons Learned and use the information to feedback to the front-end evaluation process.

There may always be some project environment variables that are elusive and for which you will not be able to easily identify unintended consequences of actions taken by the project manager, project team, sponsors, or other stakeholders. That does not mean that you should dismiss this analysis as having no value.

Remember: The more you know and understand about all the variables in the PMO and its organizational setting that can impact project team and stakeholder behavior, the quicker you can identify process improvements and achieve sustained project success. That is a sign of Maturity of your project process, and is a goal worth striving for.

24
SUMMARY

Some readers might ask the question, "In what situations other than project close can this framework and the organizational dynamics viewpoint be applied?" From my experience working with several Program Management Offices (PMOs), those who focus on contracts as the action vehicle can also apply this framework. In this case, it might be termed "Contract Closeout and Lessons Learned," but the emphasis on Significant Events and deviations between Expected and Actual Results for the contracts would be the same.

Likewise, if a pundit chose to focus on Significant Events from the 2016 Presidential Election, then this framework presented in this book could also be applied. It would be very interesting to see the list of Risks identified in such an analysis.

The organizational dynamics and dynamic complexity framework in this book that has been applied to projects as events, and patterns of behavior arising from the project environment, could also be applied to other dynamically complex situations. Appendix 3, for example, provides a detailed case study related to teen drivers. Certainly, these same concepts could be applied to debates in America concerning gun regulations and the various aspects and factors influencing deaths by guns.

I have designed this book for every project manager who sincerely wants to improve the way his or her project teams capture, document, and share project Lessons Learned. The actionability of the resulting project Lessons Learned from the framework presented in this book can improve the business processes of the project organization.

Project closeout can be a harried time for a project team. In addition to taking care of tangible deliverables and assuring customers and stakeholders that all objectives for the project were satisfied, the project team must also account for the three major areas of concern: schedule, budget, and scope. How well did the activities of project control lead to a project that was within schedule, within budget, and met the scope objectives for the project? Were all the deliverables of the quality that customers and stakeholders agreed to in the Project Charter and the early project planning meetings?

Also, project managers are always looking forward to their next project assignment. Will it be a complex project with many geographic regions or markets to manage? Will it have the resources needed to successfully carry out all the tasks at hand? Will it have the direction from the Steering Committee that it deserves?

In this book, we have seen how projects can be examined as single events with Lessons Learned defined by examining the project results and behaviors, and then drawing conclusions about what contributed to deviations from expected performance or outcomes for the individual projects.

We have also examined the situation in which a project environment may have several projects subject to that same environment, meaning that the behavior of the projects has been influenced by the structure and policies in place in that environment. We have seen that certain patterns of behavior can be identified for several projects playing in the same project space, and that conclusions can be drawn about the systemic structure of that environment. The systemic structure can then be analyzed by looking at the mental models in place as a result of the vision that people hold for the organization and its work.

I am sure there are many readers who are skeptical and asking the question, "How can you be sure that these behaviors are actually taking place? Even if I did see some performance issues with projects, I am not sure I could relate them to structure." My answer is to take some simple steps first. Assume you have five projects that are being executed in the same space, meaning they are subject to the same project environment. That is the event level. Then look for patterns of behavior among the projects. Do the project teams seem to handle a specific task or deliverable in a certain way? Does the project manager make decisions that result in outcomes he did not foresee? Understanding events and patterns of behavior are the first steps.

Also, look for recurring events that don't match expected outcomes. Usually the organization is too busy to stop and do a root-cause analysis of such recurring events. But many of these recurring events can be traced back to short-term goals or a mental model of expected behavior from management that drives the outcome. I have written extensively in my blog *Mel Bost PMO Expert* (www.melbostpmoexpert.com) about some of these behaviors and resulting outcomes, so scan the Table of Contents for my blog to pick out some of your interest. Second, look for stepped-up behavior in a particular area that doesn't seem justified. For example, as I mentioned in this book, in one PMO, they established a rule that all projects over $1 million had to go through an extensive justification and approval process that required detailed financial analysis, business case, and project charter. All projects under $1 million had an abbreviated justification and approval process consisting of a project charter and limited business case. An overwhelming number of projects were submitted in the $800,000 level. Why? Structure (or policy in this case) influenced behavior. Twenty-five $800,000 projects and five $1.5 million projects were submitted in the same time period. These are just a few examples of how PMO personnel can begin to understand PMO organizational dynamics.

With all that I have covered in this book on organizational dynamics and behavior of groups, there is growing evidence that many people in organizations are more cognizant every day of the impact that mental models and organizational culture have on behavior. In their book *REWORK*, Jason Fried and David Heinemeier Hansson, the founders of the software development and consulting firm 37 Signals, focused on several behavioral topics such as workaholics. Workaholics are often driven by their desire to be valued by the organization in which they have sensed a climate that encourages workaholism. But the rules of the game are changed now from previous times. No longer do people believe that a person can function at full energy level for 24 hours. The belief is that short energy spurts by individuals are the norm, and now people are countering the influence of organizations by rejecting the workaholic behaviors. This type of revelation will spread slowly but it will spread.

The *REWORK* authors have also stated a principle that actually goes against the grain of traditional organizational dynamics in the systems archetype Limits to Growth. Whereas, in Limits to Growth, we seek to understand and eliminate the barriers and constraints (balancing loop) opposing the growth (reinforcing loop) to sustain growth in the initiative, the authors tell us to "embrace constraints," and find new opportunities because the rules of the game have been altered. As Louis Tice once expressed in his personal development workshops, "Everyone thought it was crazy that someone would want to fly because the law of gravity dictates a set of behavior. But when the law of gravity was upended by a whole new law of aerodynamics, thoughts changed."

The type of thinking displayed in *REWORK* may lead to new organizational dynamic views of the way organizations think and act and even lead to what Peter Senge has referred to for many years in his work as the "learning organization."

How quickly this thinking will impact PMOs is another question.

Understanding the dynamics of single and multiple project situations can be difficult, but project managers need that insight to become better project managers and to take on other roles in their organizations and the larger project community that would allow improvement in performance for all projects. As I stated several times in this book, even the most experienced project manager often has difficulty at first applying the framework and documenting actionable Lessons Learned from projects. It takes repeated effort focusing on the criteria of actionability to assure oneself that the lesson learned can be truly implementable within a Continuous Process Improvement Framework.

I hope that this book has provided insights into the thought processes that support better project performance and an understanding of the principal causes of project disappointments.

Readers are encouraged to continue reading my blog *Mel Bost PMO Expert* (www.melbostpmoexpert.com) for insights into PMO structure, activity, performance, and behavior.

I also encourage readers to e-mail me to discuss how their implementation of the project Closeout and Lessons Learned framework was successful for their project organization. This dialogue with others who value project Closeout and Lessons Learned as a discipline has been invaluable to my understanding and direction for future project managers. Thank you.

Appendix 1: Project Lessons Learned Template

What was the Expected Result?	1. Examine project plans, assumptions, deliverables, risk management plans, business case, and financial case for the specific events.
What was the Actual Result?	1. Analyze actual performance versus expected performance for significant events. 2. See chapter on selection of candidates for Lessons Learned.
What is the Gap?	1. For each significant event, define the gap between expected and actual in as much detail as you can.
What is the Lesson to be Learned?	1. For each significant event, summarize in detail the Lesson to be learned. 2. Cite risk, new technology prove-out, and key factors.
Comments	

Appendix 2: A Layman's Guide to Reinforcing and Balancing Loop Behavior and the Resulting Systems Archetypes

Note: This explanation is intended for the general public's understanding of systems archetypes without the detailed stocks and flows, or mathematics associated with feedback processes. It is intended for the rapid assimilation of the material by the reader so that managers can recognize and take appropriate actions in the face of these feedback processes from organizational dynamics.

General

The systems archetypes describe common patterns of behavior in organizations.

System archetypes are highly effective tools for gaining insight into patterns of behavior, themselves reflective of the underlying "structure" of the system being studied. The archetypes can be applied in two ways—diagnostically and prospectively.

Diagnostically, archetypes help managers recognize patterns of behavior that are already present in their organizations. They serve as the means for gaining insight into the underlying systems structures from which the archetypal behavior emerges. This is the most common use of the archetype.

Archetypes are effective tools for beginning to answer the question, "Why do we keep seeing the same problems recur over time?"

Prospectively, archetypes are useful for planning. As managers formulate the means by which they expect to accomplish their organizational ends, the archetypes can be applied to test whether policies and structures under consideration may be altering the organizational structure in such manner as to produce the archetypal behavior. If managers find this to be the case, they can take remedial action before the changes are adopted and embedded in the organization's structure.

From my experience, archetypes can be highly effective when examining Program Management Office (PMO) and IT Project Office organizational structure.

Specifics

There are two distinct types of feedback processes from which systems archetypes are derived: reinforcing feedback processes and balancing feedback processes. Feedback means that the organization reacts to the initiatives of the PMO.

Reinforcing (or amplifying) feedback processes are the engines of growth. Whenever you are in a situation where things are growing, you can be sure that reinforcing feedback is at work.

Balancing (or stabilizing) feedback processes operate whenever there is a goal-oriented behavior or a barrier or resistance to growth.

In an organization such as a PMO, reinforcing feedback can occur when the PMO initiates an action, and communication to the organization is positive—meaning the organization accepts the direction and acts accordingly. Growth is the result because the feedback to the PMO indicates that they can continue the activity with the expected result being an increase in acceptance by the organization, and therefore more compliance, and more growth.

In an organization such as a PMO, balancing feedback processes can occur when there is a goal to be reached, or when resistance to the directive of the PMO initiative is encountered. This resistance or barrier to growth is encountered when a reinforcing loop encounters a balancing loop. After initial acceptance of the PMOs directive, there may come a time when the goal is being approached or that organizational resistance to the PMO directive is encountered.

Limits to Growth

A Limits to Growth system archetype consists of a reinforcing loop and a balancing loop. The reinforcing loop is active, as when a PMO initiates an activity or program and the organization accepts and acts positively on the initiative. Growth begins. At some point, the balancing loop is activated by some resistance or barrier to the initiative by the organization. What was once seen as a growth scenario then becomes a limited growth scenario, with the activity approaching some asymptotic level. Actions by the PMO to recognize the resistance or barriers can lead to increased growth again if the PMO is successful at identifying the resistance.

Tragedy of the Commons

This systems archetype was named for a scenario from old England, where people settled around a bountiful grassy area (the Commons) and raised sheep. More people recognized the bountiful nature of the grassy Commons and settled around the Commons area. Eventually, the sheep overgrazed the Commons so that the sheep population declined due to no more grass (the Tragedy). This systems archetype is often present in situations where the PMO is situated near a specialized group, such as an IT Infrastructure Security group. In defining project team makeup, often the PMO would "borrow" resources from the Security group for certain aspects of the project. The intent was to control costs. However, as soon as a security breach occurred at a crucial project time, the Security resources were pulled back and were not available to the project. As more projects began to use the Security resources, a Tragedy of the Commons scenario emerged.

Growth and Underinvestment

This systems archetype reflects a standard of performance at some point in the organization, in which the behavior of the organization takes into account its feedback processes. The standard may be implicit or explicit, meaning it may be a stated, documented standard, or an unstated/undocumented standard that is nevertheless understood by the actors to be in effect.

Reinforcing and balancing loops operate in the Growth and Underinvestment scenario, but there is also a side loop that seeks to satisfy the standard. If the standard is maintained in the face of growth, then the balancing loop will retard the growth to be consistent with the standard. If the organization recognizes that its growth may require a reassessment of the standard to a higher level, then the growth may continue if the standard is raised. This allows for development within the organization based on the higher-level standard being sought.

Often, however, the organization recognizes growth without recognizing the standard controlling the growth. In this case, underinvestment occurs and the growth and underinvestment scenario plays out.

This scenario is sometimes seen in PMOs when an internal goal of controlling project costs results in the project teams' anticipating the use of resources that are not dedicated to the projects, but which are part of the larger organization (such as local geographic resources or resources associated with a specialized group like Security). An underinvestment in the resources needed at the right time and in the right quantity results eventually in increased cost and time to complete the projects.

Accidental Adversaries

This archetype describes behavior between two parties who have everything to gain by working together, but end up sabotaging the end result because they each focus on their internal goals at the expense of the larger enterprise. It was first identified 20 years ago in the relationship between Procter and Gamble (P&G) and Wal-Mart. P&G had a rigorous manufacturing schedule for their consumer products, while Wal-Mart's deep discounting and promotional offers undermined P&G's manufacturing schedule to the point where the two companies were always at odds in supply and demand.

This archetype shows up today in situations where a husband and wife may be in conflict, two strategic partners may be in a long-term relationship, and even in the case of two countries engaged in war.

The systems archetype includes both reinforcing and balancing loops internally and a larger external overriding loop explaining the overall behavior of the partnership. This behavior often shows up in PMOs and IT Project Offices, where a management consultant is employed to ramp up maturity of the PMO group, while the PMO group tries to develop its own identity through unique processes and methodology internally consistent with its business context.

There are many other systems archetypes at work in organizations every day. The few mentioned here are illustrative of the reinforcing and balancing feedback mechanisms at play today.

Appendix 3: Systems Thinking and Organizational Dynamics Example—Teen Drivers

The issue of teen drivers and deadly crashes is a dynamically complex situation. In situations that are dynamically complex, cause and effect are subtle, and the effects manifest over much longer time periods and differ depending on time frame, locations, populations, and so forth. Many times, doing the obvious thing does not produce the obvious, desired outcome. On the part of the parents, doing the obvious thing in this situation may be placing continued trust on the teen driver's ability to make choices in complex driving situations. The key is to see not only the linear cause and effect links but also the interrelationships of the variables and the processes as a whole.

Range of Variables for Teen Driver Environment Summary:

Teen Drivers and/or Passenger(s)

- Mobility
- Independence
- Complex vehicle environment

LEVEL OF REASONING	TOPIC	DESCRIPTION
High leverage and high complexity	Vision	All of these levels are informed by vision and commitment. The key question at this level is "what are we trying to create?" or "what do we seem to be creating?" These aspirations, stated or unstated, exert a powerful on the events, patterns, systemic structure, and mental models working in any given situation. Keys to solving this dynamically complex situation involve all of the following: • Changing parent's attitudes about inconvenience versus saving lives • Public support for raising driving age must be apparent before politicians consider raising driving age • Scientific conclusions about teen driver immaturity with regard to the consequences of their driving actions must impact both parents and politicians A clear vision has not been articulated for this dynamically complex situation. Although parents want to place trust in the ability of their teen to handle the complex driving situations, the multitasking structure overwhelms the teen's ability to perform to acceptable standards. Driving as an emotional experience seems to defy the rational and objective statistics that would limit the mobility of the teen-driving population. The fact that there are publicized Lessons Learned from the analysis of data and statistics about the patterns of behavior does not automatically imply that improvement will be made to the system that describes this scenario. The systems structure tends to resist changes based on feedback and only through concerted efforts in the decentralized systems that make up the larger system will long-lasting changes be made. (If this was a physical system with such publicized Lessons Learned, improvements would be almost immediate.)
	Mental models	Although impacted by the publicity surrounding accident statistics, individual family units often approach teen driving as individual family decisions depending on the family circumstances. Rational and objective data concerning teen fatalities in accidents are therefore of limited value in the ultimate decisions, because the decisions are driven so much by emotion and family desires. There is evidence, however, that this structure is maturing, with increased changes in the type of vehicles being sought by families for teen drivers and the increased supervision of teen drivers by parents and state actions regarding licensing. Possible mental models: • Risky behavior in teen years is expected, and driving is no exception. • Culture supports freedom of mobility. • "Really, the only way to get experience is to get out and drive."

(Continued)

(Continued)

(Continued)

LEVEL OF REASONING	TOPIC	DESCRIPTION
		• "Responsible teen drivers should not be punished for the mistakes of the small fraction that cause deadly crashes."
		• "Parents are more concerned with inconvenience of having to drive their teens than about saving lives."
		• "This happens elsewhere but not in my household."
		• "Driving or the ability to drive is an experience driven by emotions."
		Observations impacting mental models:
		• "Some states will license even teens who got speeding tickets while driving with a learner's permit."
		• "Police will look on enforcement of graduated licensing as a priority depending on what importance the public puts on it."
	Systemic structure	A basic driving and motility framework supports this structure with the following components:
		• Licensing of drivers
		• Training (levels vary by region with some not requiring training)
		• Laws for driving and mobility in vehicles (when, where, how)
		• Interpretation and enforcement of laws
		• Vehicle safety equipment and requirement for usage (seat belts, etc.)
		• Vehicle safety standards for rollover
		• Vehicle configuration
		Decentralized, fragmented framework:
		• States individually responsible for licensing and enforcement.
		• Role of insurance institute and National Highway Traffic Safety Administration (NHTSA) unclear.
		• Parents attitudes often let teens skirt the laws or provides trust in teen ability to navigate complex driving scenarios.
		Lack of compliance with standards:
		• Unlicensed drivers driving.
		• Lax enforcement of speeding or alcohol laws.
		• Weak seat belt laws.
		• Graduated licensing rules poorly enforced or riddled with loopholes.
		• State laws often don't restrict behavior that is linked to many teen fatalities.

(*Continued*)

LEVEL OF REASONING	TOPIC	DESCRIPTION
		Failure to incorporate Lessons Learned feedback for improvement
		• New Jersey, which has long barred 16-year-olds from having unrestricted driver's licenses, for years, has had one of the lowest teen fatality rates in the USA.
		• Teen fatalities have declined in states with graduated licensing programs and restrictions on teen transport and when they can drive (nighttime curfew).
		• Insurance Institute: "As the proportion of 16-year-olds in the USA with driver's licenses has declined from a decade ago, so has the proportion of 16-year-olds involved in fatal crashes."
		The increase in the number of states over the past few years that placed added restrictions on teen drivers indicates a maturing structure with regard to the problem and its consequences for the public and for families.
		Systemic Structure: The multitasking requirements placed on the driver in this complex driver/vehicle/environment does not match the competency level and capability of the driver whose decisions are driven by emotion and whose brain is not mature enough to consider the consequences of driving actions. Parents and highway traffic administrators continually place trust in the ability of driver to perform in this multitasking environment. This could be considered an example of a growth and underinvestment archetype in which not enough investment can be made in the capability of the driver (due to constraints and limitations) to meet increasing levels of demand of complex driving situations.
Patterns of behavior		Patterns of behavior were established for the fatal vehicle crashes by *USA Today* through analysis of crash statistics:
		• More than two-thirds of fatal single vehicle teen crashes involved nighttime driving or at least one passenger aged 16–19.
		• Nearly three-fourths of the drivers in those crashes were male.
		• Sixteen-year-old drivers were the riskiest of all—their rate of involvement in fatal crashes was nearly five times to that of drivers aged 20 and older.
		Conclusions were that the risk to teen lives rises when:
		• A 16-year-old is at the wheel.
		• They are riding with other teens.
		• They are in teen-driven cars after dark.
		• The young driver loses control.
		• They are in an unsuitable vehicle (from a rollover rating perspective).
		• They drive in more dangerous regions such as rural, tree-lined streets or in southern states with lax enforcement of alcohol or speeding laws.

(*Continued*)

(Continued)

LEVEL OF REASONING	TOPIC	DESCRIPTION
Low leverage and low complexity	Events	*USA Today* examined all the deadly vehicle crashes involving 16- to 19-year-old drivers in 2003. Approximately 3,500 teenagers died in teen-driven vehicles in the USA in that year. The single events were vehicles driven by teens with outcomes resulting in crashes and death. The events were not close in space and time but dispersed throughout the USA over the entire year. This tends to lead us initially to an analysis on a case-by-case basis with no link established among the events at this lowest level of observation. The cause and effect of a single crash could have been analyzed as, for example, "excessive speed resulting in death of the driver and/or passenger (s)."

Family

- Mobility
- Convenience/inconvenience
- Stability
- Attitudes
- Vehicle configuration

State

- Licensing
- Enforcement
- Interpretation and judgment

Automobile manufacturers

- Compliance
- Sales
- Vehicle configuration

Government and other agencies

- Insurance Institute
  - Insurance
  - Safety statistics input to insurance and insurability
  - NHTSA
    - Safety
    - Prevention

The reason for listing the range of variables is that some of these or combinations of these may be the key leveraging variables for improving total system performance. By changing certain key leveraging variables, the structure may be changed, which will in turn affect the pattern of behavior.

Appendix 4: Project Lessons Learned from the Panama Canal Experiences

In the summer of 2011, I had the opportunity to spend 10 days with the project managers, engineers, and contract administrators of the Panama Canal Authority Construction Division teaching the project Closeout and Lessons Learned process presented in this book. It was a great experience that provided me with many insights into project and risk management practices at work.

The Panama Canal Authority was engaged in a $5 billion Expansion Program to allow larger seagoing vessels to be accommodated by the canal. The program sought to build a third set of locks and navigation channels along with other infrastructure to facilitate the movement of vessels. At the time of my work there, the Construction Division had completed several large excavation and construction projects in support of the expansion, and they were eager to capture, document, and share lessons learned from those projects using my framework and a dashboard-reporting tool.

The original construction, upgrading, and expansion projects for the Panama Canal over the past 150 years have provided a rich collection of project lessons for study, review, and enrichment of current project management literature. In early 1850s, many nations around the world talked about the desirability of a transportation connection between the Atlantic and Pacific Oceans. The Isthmus of Panama became a constant talking point and a focus of effort to complete this transportation connection.

However, the story of achieving this transportation connection is also a story of the advancement of project and risk management techniques and of technology development to support the huge efforts. It is also a story of the utilization of human resources at enormous costs, including the loss of many lives, to achieve the objective. Approximately 25,000 people died during the French project, the first attempt to build the canal in the late 1860s, and an additional 5,000 during the U.S. project, the second (and successful) attempt to build the canal in the early 1900s.

Since this book addresses project and risk management as well as organization and structure and the impact on behavior and actions of project teams, I want to summarize some of the Panama Canal project work as examples to show how application of the Lessons Learned and Risk Processes can assist in your future project work.

The First Panama Canal Project—French Consortium

The success of the French in building the Suez Canal in Egypt in 1869 made them the instant front-runners in the development of the Panama Canal. The diplomat who led the Suez Canal development was not technically trained. A commercial venture was formed with investors to pursue the Panama Canal development. However, the scope was ill-defined and project requirements not fully understood throughout the effort. Panama's terrain and climate differ markedly from Egypt, and none of the French took this into account with their work. Canals before this point in time had generally been handled by manual power with animals used to open and close any canal doors. The Panama rain forest also created wet and dry seasons that were not factored into the project planning by the French.

An Engineering Congress was convened in Paris in 1879 to facilitate the sharing of ideas regarding new canal development. The Congress covered many options for transportation, including a lock and dam system similar to the final choice of a solution for Panama.

Originally, the scope of the canal was to build a sea-level canal. However, after many years of study, it was decided that a sea-level canal was not feasible due to the amount of excavation and dirt removal required.

After much talk and investigation throughout the 1870s, the French project was launched in 1882. After taking a closer look at actual Panama conditions, cost estimates were increased many times over the next few years and little progress was shown in actually constructing a canal. Much excavation work was completed, but the project was canceled in 1889 as investors abandoned the consortium group and it fell into bankruptcy. This was such a failure that it has often been cited as the reason for the fall of the French government in 1892. Scandal was rampant.

The French bout with diseases such as yellow fever and malaria also resulted in many worker deaths. Estimates of total deaths on this project were as high as 25,000.

It was almost 15 years until the next full-scale effort was pursued regarding a canal connecting the Atlantic and Pacific Oceans.

The Second Panama Canal Project—U.S. Sponsorship

When President Theodore Roosevelt came to office in 1901, he saw the creation and control of the Panama Canal as the key to America, projecting itself as a world power. "If we are to hold our own in the struggle for supremacy," Roosevelt insisted, "we must build the canal." With Roosevelt's backing, Panamanians claimed their independence from Colombia in 1903 after a bloodless revolution. The United States and Panama signed a treaty giving the U.S. sovereignty over the "Canal Zone," a 440-square-mile area stretching across the isthmus.

Over the next decade, engineers, politicians, and laborers involved in this epic undertaking faced incredible hardships: bureaucratic inefficiencies, wild terrain, extreme weather, outbreaks of yellow fever and malaria, and generally poor working conditions. Three different engineers would take on the project during its time. In 1904, John F. Wallace came to the isthmus with an order from President Roosevelt to "make the dirt fly." When Wallace left Panama after only a year, he had accomplished little and left morale along the isthmus low. In July 1905, John Stevens took over as chief engineer. He first sought to rebuild the railroad—a project that both organized the entire endeavor and allowed for the development of innovations that would prove crucial to the success of the canal's construction. By the time he finished, the railroad functioned as a giant conveyor belt for excavated spoil, shifting continuously to accommodate the work as it progressed.

With the railroad system improved, Stevens concentrated on the Culebra Mountain, the highest point of the Isthmus. He quickly realized that digging a sea-level cut through the mountain while battling the formidable current of the Chagres River would be impossible. He supported a new plan with a system of locks, a massive dam to control the Chagres, and a giant artificial lake 85 feet above sea level. Implementing this plan exhausted Stevens, who resigned in February 1907.

Colonel George Washington Goethals became the third and final chief engineer for the Panama Canal. Goethals' stepped up the pace of production, refusing to negotiate with strikers and ordering labor to continue around the clock; at any given time, day or night, thousands of men were working in the canal. The rigorous production schedule yielded visible progress by 1911, improving worker morale. In May of 1913, steam shovels finally met at the middle of the cut. Soon workers sealed the last spillway at Gatun dam, allowing the water of Gatun Lake to rise to its full height. After demolishing the dikes at either end of the canal, the Atlantic and Pacific Oceans rushed inland, and the final stretch of the Culebra Cut was flooded. On August 15, 1914, the Panama Canal was finally opened to the public.

After more than a decade of struggle, successful completion of the Panama Canal established the United States as a global power in commerce and technology at the dawn of the 20th century.

The successful chief engineers on the Second Panama Canal project had railroad construction/operation, and dam and bridge-building backgrounds. This was a major factor in the success of the project because these men understood construction in very rough terrain as well as the importance of communication to the success of projects.

Although the French project, on the other hand, had little or no project management or risk management principles, the Second Canal project paralleled the birth and rise of rapid usage of project management and project risk management principles. Principal risks identified for the U.S. project were the following:

1. Disease
2. Mud slides

3. Constant use of explosives
4. Mechanical challenges of lock development
5. Electrical and control systems development

When the second Panama Canal project was finished in 1914, the canal's operation had been so widely anticipated that many problems with its operations were overshadowed by the desire to keep the canal operational. However, one problem, namely, the source of the water to fill the locks, persisted that had not been addressed earlier. If risk analysis techniques had been applied early, it might have been addressed, but it was not.

Filling the canal locks with water was accomplished by taking water from Gatun Lake and then draining the water from the locks to the sea following each operation. This was okay as long as the rainy season kept Gatun Lake to a level that the extraction of water for the locks was not a problem. However, there were some seasons where lake levels fell and operation of the canal was ceased due to lack of sufficient water. Operation of U.S. Naval vessels moving between Atlantic and Pacific Oceans was adversely affected by these events.

As a result, in 1935 a new dam was constructed upstream from Gatun Lake to ensure a continuous supply of water to the lock system. Some students of the Panama Canal development have identified this situation as an enterprise risk because of the impact of overall operations of the canal.

Technology Development Aspects of the Projects

The second half of the 19th century was a time of expansion and great technological advancement. Americans built the Brooklyn Bridge and completed the Transcontinental Railroad. Development of electric motors and electric systems was highlighted by three-phase electric motor development in the late 1880s. This laid the groundwork for electric system development in the U.S. Panama Canal effort.

Once the scope of the project was better understood, including the difficulties presented by the formidable terrain of Panama and the other obstacles to be overcome in constructing a canal, efforts were focused on the technology development that was required to complete the locks and the electrical and control systems for the

Panama Canal. Both presented tremendous challenges throughout the project.

The Panama Canal project included one of the largest and most important electrical installations in the world early in the 20th century. The use of 1,022 electric motors, with an installed capacity of 28,290 horsepower largely replaced the steam and water powered equipment then in common use. Reliability and safety were also engineered into the innovative electrical control system, enabling remote lock operation from a central location.

The electrical installations made possible the construction of the canal, and, more importantly, provided the electrical power required for the operation of the canal for the remainder of the 20th Century.

The construction of the canal was considered the world's greatest engineering work at the time. The project was begun by the French in 1876 with the formation of a society to survey Central America for the purpose of building an interoceanic canal. It was determined that Panama would provide the best opportunity for success. The first shovel of soil was turned on January 1, 1880. By 1884, there were as many as 19,000 workers on site, but they suffered many obstacles, including disease and funding, and by 1889, all activity ceased.

The United States canal construction began in 1904, after it acquired the French company's assets and concessions. Sanitation was one of the first issues to be addressed and solved. Communications were improved with new telegraph and telephone systems. It was estimated (by John F. Stevens, Chief Engineer) that it would take a minimum of 8 years to complete a lock canal (1914) and a sea-level canal in 18 years (1924).

Electric power was chosen as the most dependable and economical form of power for the operation of the construction plants for the locks, with their cement mixers, stone crushers, cranes, cable ways, automatic locomotives, pumps, etc. Electrical engineer Edward Schildhauer, AIEE Fellow (1913), designed the powerful gate operating mechanism. Each 20-foot diameter gate is powered by an electric motor. Lock operations required over 1,000 electric motors, as all controls were electric.

Electric motors had already proven to be the most reliable form of power to drive the pumps and other equipment. Alternative forms of power, such as animal, compressed air, and steam had been previously considered and discarded. All the power required for the operation of the two Construction Plants, one located at Gatun and the other at Miraflores, was generated on site. Each plant was fitted with three Curtis steam turbines, 1.5 MW each. They operated at 2,200 V, 25 cycles, and were connected through a 44 kV double circuit electric line that crossed the isthmus.

After its opening in August of 1914, the new Gatun Hydroelectric Plant provided the electric power required for the operation of the canal. The construction plant and its steam turbines located at Gatun were shut down; the one at Miraflores was kept as a backup source of power in case of transmission problems.

The electrical and control system was designed for remote and centralized operation so that various parts of the canal could be operated from a single vantage point where the control system was located.

After 88 years of uninterrupted service, the canal continues to provide highly reliable service due, in large part, to its electrical equipment.

During the years 1914 through 1933, there were a number of improvements to the canal. In 1933, the U.S. Army Corps of Engineers were called in to make major improvements. They worked until 1939 when they were redeployed to the World War efforts. Much of their work was not completed, however, and many excavation and concrete improvements were left to the jungle growth and deterioration over the years.

The Panama Canal Expansion Project which began in 2009 faced this jungle growth condition head on and often informed contractors that "unknown site conditions" was a major risk. My Lessons Learned Courses in 2011 were met with much enthusiasm and participants used the Framework instantly.

Timeline for Events Impacting Panama Canal Projects

1855—Panama Railroad Completed Linking Atlantic and Pacific Oceans

1869—Suez Canal completed by French group

1876—First Panama Canal Project started by French consortium as a commercial venture with investors

1879—Engineering Congress convened in Paris to focus on canal development

1885—Paris regarded as center of engineering excellence for western world; best engineering schools in world located in Paris

1889—First Panama Canal Project Canceled; consortium bankrupt

1903—Panama Republic formed from Colombia; U.S. granted sovereignty over the Canal Zone

1904—Initiation of Second Panama Canal Project sponsored by U.S. Government

1914—Project completion date for Second Panama Canal Project

1933—U.S. Army Corps of Engineers begins Panama project to construct new lock system

1939—U.S. Army Corps of Engineers redeployed to World War II; Panama Canal work ceased

1999—Turnover date of Panama Canal to Panama Republic

2009—Panama Canal Expansion Program Consortium formed

2016—Completion of the Panama Canal Expansion Program

Appendix 5: Capability Maturity Model Background and Levels of Maturity

Capability Maturity Model

Introduction: In 1979, Philip Crosby introduced a maturity grid/matrix applicable to organizations in his book *Quality Is Free*. It was known as the "Management Maturity Grid," and described a progression of maturity in organizations related to management moving from "Ad Hoc" activities and "quality," to a mature state or environment in which Quality was embraced as the norm for all employees. Feedback was employed to improve activities and ensure quality.

In the 1980s, IBM's Watts Humphrey initiated software development work based on the Management Maturity Grid. Over the past decades, this work has been called "Capability Maturity Model" and has been extended from strictly software development to process development and process maturity for organizations generally.

Capability Maturity Model Levels of Maturity

Level One—Initial (Ad Hoc): The process is characterized as Ad Hoc and occasionally even "chaotic." Few processes are defined and success depends on individual effort and heroics.

Level Two—Repeatable: Basic processes are established for a few routine activities. The organization is beginning to understand "process."

Level Three—Defined: The processes are defined and integrated into a standard process for the organization.

Level Four—Managed: Measures of performance for the processes and their outputs are used to improve the processes. Process is embraced and a standard way of operating.

Level Five—Optimized: Continuous process improvement is enabled by quantitative feedback from the processes and from piloting innovative ideas and technology.

Appendix 6: Research as a Major Process

Project Management Knowledge Areas Applied to Research

The Project Management Institute uses the Project Management Body of Knowledge to describe knowledge areas that should be covered in a project. When applied to research, the knowledge areas are as follows:

1. Research integration
   a. Research project charter
   b. Research scope statement
   c. Research management plan
   d. Research execution management
   e. Research control

   Research integration is essential for cases where your research outputs will feed into other projects for the purpose of achieving an overall integrated system.
2. Research scope management
   a. Focused statement of research
   b. Research cost/benefit analysis
   c. Research constraints
   d. Research work breakdown structure
   e. Research activity breakdown structure
   f. Research change control

Research scope management is essential for ensuring your research does not grow needlessly and endlessly. The fear of a student is that a research advisor will add additional requirements and expectations.

3. Research time management
4. Research cost management
5. Research quality management
6. Research human resources management
7. Research communications management
8. Research *risk* management
    a. Research risk identification
    b. Research risk analysis
    c. Research risk mitigation
    d. Research risk contingency
9. Research *procurement* management
    a. Research material selection
    b. Research vendor prequalification
    c. Research contract types
    d. Research contract risk assessment
    e. Research contract negotiation
    f. Research contract change orders

Potential Research Project Risks

1. Integration risk: dependencies
2. Vendor risk
    a. Contract
    b. Performance
3. Hypothesis test risk
4. Data collection risks
    a. Collection
    b. Assessment/analysis
    c. Interpretation
5. Resources risk
    a. Availability
    b. Mix

6. Technology development risks
   a. Controllable risks
   b. Uncontrollable risks
7. Methodology risks
   a. Textual analysis
   b. Spatial analysis
   c. Network analysis
   d. Others

Appendix 7: Scenarios Where Lessons Learned Can Positively Impact Performance and Outcomes

1. Elections (presidential, gubernatorial, congressional, etc.)
2. Weather (hurricanes, snowstorms, etc.)
3. Academics
4. Team sports (baseball, football, basketball, etc.)
5. Individual sports
6. Medical results
7. Automotive product development
8. Biopharmaceutical development
9. Construction projects
10. Food preparation
11. Food services
12. Olympic events

Epilogue

The seeds for this book were planted when I was six or seven years old. But then, I had no experience.

I had an idea for a fanciful book about a railroad operating over a flowing river which was obscured from the sight of the surrounding area by virtue of the tall trees that lined the river bank. I developed several crayon drawings of the railroad and wrote several pages in pencil on lined looseleaf notebook paper. No one seemed to care or pay much attention.

Then in middle school, I would often return home on Friday evenings from the local high school football game and compose an article about the game using the same style and layout as the Sunday paper. Often, I would write myself into the game as the hero who scored the winning touchdown. It was fun to read these accounts back to myself. No one seemed to care or pay much attention.

Then, when I was ten years old, something significant happened. Growing up in Concord, North Carolina, there was an activity that I really enjoyed each week in the summer. It was watching the televised "Baseball Game of the Week."

Now, you have to understand that baseball on television then was very different from baseball on television today. There was no WGN in Chicago to carry the Cubs games. There was no TBS in Atlanta to carry the Braves games. There was no ESPN to analyze the game of baseball from 40 different angles.

There was simply one station—CBS—that carried whichever game it chose to cover, usually from the northeast and, most often, from Yankee Stadium featuring the New York Yankees.

Go figure!

Every Saturday, I was so excited for the 1:00 PM broadcast that I was actually seated in front of the television, with my favorite sandwich and beverage, at 12:30 PM waiting for the game.

As a result, I started watching a weekly series sponsored by the National Association of Manufacturers, entitled "Industry on Parade", which preceded the baseball game. The series was a showcase of the latest manufacturing technologies and new approaches to emerging industries, like plastics, after World War II.

Although they did not emphasize its importance in the weekly shows, "Industry on Parade" was a great introductory course in Process. In fact, it was probably the best course I ever took in Process, as defined by the traditional Michael Hammer definition of "an organized group of related activities that together create customer value." That includes my coursework while earning my undergraduate and graduate degrees in science, engineering, and business.

What "Industry on Parade" did for me was to imprint on my mind a visual image of a specific set of activities, which together led to a finished product, service, outcome, or goal. The experience had such a profound effect on me that my approach to almost any situation from that point forward was to look for the Process behind the actual description of the events and activities.

When I was in graduate school at both Georgia Tech and the University of Michigan, I studied nuclear reactor feedback and control theory. This was in essence a process whereby inputs to the process would lead to output and some of these outputs, because they were part of the larger system within which the process operated, would create feedback processes, which in turn affected the process outputs as much as the original inputs did. I began to appreciate the way physical systems subject to feedback processes could create enhanced outputs by virtue of the feedback. In essence, the networked components of a physical system can communicate with each other to produce results and outputs determined by the behavior of the system.

When I began my career with Ford Motor Company, I became part of a large organizational system with components that were networked together to form a real system. That's when I first began to see the relationship structure influences behavior.

Throughout my career in project management working in IT Project Offices as well as Program Management Offices, I began to see the organizational dynamics at play in feedback processes within the organization.

This influence of organizational dynamics in revealing why organizations behave as they do and why people react to each other as they do became a lifelong interest to me. This book is the result of that interest.

Glossary

Every industry, discipline, and community has its own unique terminology to define and describe the activities and processes of the entity. The project community is no different. The following terms and phrases are used in this community and should be reviewed by the reader to clarify any questions concerning the interpretations in this book.

Accidental adversaries—A systems archetype in which two parties or groups who should be in harmony with regard to their actions and behavior to create good outcomes for both instead resort to short-term actions and subvert the performance of the group.

Actionable—The definition and documentation of an improvement or lesson learned in such a complete way that others in the organization who are knowledgeable about the process can take action to make the necessary improvements in the process.

Activity—A component of work performed during the course of a project or process.

Artificial intelligence—The application of analysis to knowledge management systems that facilitates decision making regarding data elements and information.

Augmented intelligence—see Artificial intelligence.

Benchmarking—Using a standard against which measurements or comparisons can be made.

Best practices—In an industry, those practices that are recognized as providing excellent results for whatever institution decides to employ the practices; in a specific organization, those practices that have been used time after time to produce outstanding results will continue to be employed because of their potential for success.

Bias, confirmational—A perspective expressed by a project team member that basically reinforces a previously held belief by that team member despite other expressed perspectives that more closely mirror the scenario description.

Business continuity—The process or profession dealing with the avoidance of disruption to business functions.

Capabilities (distinctive)—The things that a company excels at doing time and time again.

Capability—The combination of people processes, technology, and organization that allows an organization or individual to deliver intended outcomes. The blueprint covers all of those components, but not separately. It determines how they will fit together. There is also an accompanying plan that specifies the people who will build pieces of the capability, the targets and incentives that will govern their actions, and a timetable for implementation.

Capability maturity model—A description of the states through which organizations evolve as they define, implement, measure, control, and improve their processes. This model provides a guide for selecting process improvement strategies.

Continuous process improvement—(1) A methodology for feeding back results, insights, or Lessons Learned to define improvements for a process, which are then put into practice to improve the process. (2) A condition or state of mind in which the people responsible for process performance continually update the process.

Deliverables—Specific and identifiable products of a project.

Design thinking—An approach to innovation that focuses on the physical, emotional, social, and cognitive needs of stakeholders or clients. It has also been called "human-centered innovation."

Dynamics—A condition introduced into Process by virtue of "time" and the changes in process elements and components with time.

Emergency response—A process or business function that addresses emergencies.

Emerging markets—Countries that have some characteristics of a developed market but, in general, lack some basic functions that would merit fully developed status.

Event—In the single project case, a described occurrence. In the multiple project case, a "project."

Fact—An identifiable, descriptive statement that is irrefutable.

Gap—A measurable difference between two statements.

Innovation—The process of turning or converting "new ideas" into "valued results and outcomes" for an organization or an individual.

Innovation PMO—A Program Management Office designed to capitalize on feedback from customers and suppliers, with internal processes designed to capitalize on innovation capabilities, and providing for the incorporation of forward thought.

Integrative thinking—An approach to projects that attempts to create win-win solutions rather than compromise solutions. It tries to include more insightful variables and new architecture elements.

Lessons learned—Experiences or insights that can be used to improve a process.

Lessons learned (project)—Experiences or insights from a specific project that can be used to improve a process.

Limits to growth—A systems archetype in which continued efforts focused on an initiative do not result in continued and expected productivity and improvements in outcomes.

Method—A reasonably complete set of rules and criteria that establishes a precise and repeatable way of performing a task and arriving at a desired result.

Methodology—A collection of methods, procedures, and standards that define an integrated synthesis of engineering approaches to the development of a product.

Organizational dynamics—A field of study related to how people in large companies and organizations behave and react to each other and how the organization can be modified to work more effectively.

Patterns of behavior—Similarities of behavior by project individuals or project teams that may be the result of the structure of the project environment.

Perspectives—Viewpoints about a scenario or situation that rely heavily on an individual's internal interpretation of life and truth.

Process—A set of activities or tasks which, when performed in a specific sequence or order, produce a desired outcome or result.

Process improvement—An update to a process-based PM feedback from process performance.

Program—A group of projects related in some manner and which contribute to a collective outcome.

Project—An initiative that generally has the following characteristics:

1. Specific start and finish dates
2. Dedicated human and physical resources
3. Defined scope and deliverables that are intended to produce an outcome
4. Defined activities and schedule to support the effort
5. Allocated or assigned budget related to the scope of the project

Project charter—A document issued by the project initiator or sponsor that formally authorizes the execution of a project and provides the project manager with the authority to apply organizational resources to project activities.

Project environment—The environment created in a project organization by the structure that the organization employs to govern its behavior, actions, and performance.

Project management body of knowledge (PMBOK)—Areas of competency or expertise that are recognized by the Project Management Institute that are necessary for management of a project.

Project management institute (PMI)—The international organization that addresses standards and practices for the discipline of project management.

Project/program management office (PMO)—A project group or organization within a larger firm or organization that is usually charged with developing standards, processes, and policies for project management, and which ensures that consistency and repeatability are maintained for the firm's projects. PMOs are usually found in more mature project organizations that firmly believe that projects turn strategy into action for the firm.

Reflection—An activity of looking back at past experiences and actions and their impact on life and business processes.

Reframing—Restating a situation or scenario to highlight additional relevant facts and perspectives that may lead to a different interpretation of the situation or scenario.

Research—An application of the scientific method, which begins with a hypothesis, proceeds to the collection of data, which then requires analysis and interpretation, and finally concludes with an assessment of the hypothesis.

Risk—An event, which, if triggered, generally leads to adverse effects and outcomes for a process.

Risk, controllable—Those components of risk in project or new product development, for which the project or development team has special expertise or prior experience that can be applied to control risk factors or lessen their impact/likelihood during the project.

Risk management plan—A general plan for an organization that addresses potential risks.

Risk management plan (project)—A plan developed for a specific project that consists of risk assessment and identification, risk mitigation plans, triggers, and potential outcomes.

Risk mitigation plan—A plan, which is part of a risk management plan, that identifies potential responses to a risk if and when the risk is triggered.

Risk, uncontrollable—Those components of risk in project or new product development for which the project or development team has no special expertise or prior experience in handling. It may also represent unforeseen risks in project or product development that may occur during the project from sources unfamiliar to the project or product teams.

Scientific method—A method in which a problem is identified, relevant data is gathered, a hypothesis is formulated from the data, and the hypothesis is empirically tested.

Stakeholders—People who share an interest in, derive a value from, or require a process, initiative, or deliverable.

Structure—Policies, standards, processes, practices, and procedures that have been put in place by an organization and that may influence the behavior of the individuals in that organization.

Sustainability—A quality or condition of a state or process which seeks to strike a balance between the needs and resource utilization of current populations and those of future populations.

Sustainability implications of process—Processes require resources for implementation and value creation. How efficiently these resources are used or how the processes utilize resources that have sustainability implications. Other considerations are sharing resources and process improvements.

System—Any technology that is a dependency of a business function, including any combination of software and hardware.

Systems archetype—Discernible, identifiable, and recurring behaviors in an organization that result from the systems feedback to actions and activities of the group.

Systems thinking—A perspective of viewing scenarios by utilizing feedback from the initiative recipient to determine future initiatives.

Task—Steps that must be taken to accomplish a process or function.

Technology—The application of science and/or engineering in accomplishing some particular objective.

Technology development—An innovation process that uses technology to create valuable end products or services.

Threats—Possible sources of negative impact to organizations. They may be natural, accidental, or man-made.

Trigger—A situation or scenario that raises a risk to a level of consciousness that dictates a response from the organization.

References

Abramo, L. and Maltzman, R. 2017. *Bridging the PM Competency Gap*. J. Ross Publishing, Fort Lauderdale, FL.

Brown, T. 2009. *Change by Design*. Harper Business, New York.

Cardoza, B. 2007. *Building a Business Impact Analysis (BIA) Process: A Hands-On Blueprint*. K&M Publishers, Tulsa, OK.

Clark, R. 2004. *The Excellent 11: Qualities Teachers and Parents Use to Motivate, Inspire, and Educate Children*. Hyperion Press, Westport, CT.

Covey, S. 1991. *Principle Centered Leadership*. Summit Books, New York.

Crosby, P. 1979. *Quality Is Free: The Art of Making Quality Certain: How to Manage Quality—So That It Becomes a Source of Profit for Your Business*. Mc-Graw Hill, New York.

"Deadly Teen Auto Crashes Show a Pattern." *USA Today*, March 1, 2005.

"Driving to the Funeral." *Newsweek*, June 11, 2007.

Engemann, K. J. and Henderson, D. M. 2012. *Business Continuity and Risk Management: Essentials of Organizational Resilience*. Rothstein Associates, Inc., Brookfield, CT.

Epstein, D. and Maltzman, R. 2014. *Project Workflow Management: A Business Process Approach*. J. Ross Publishing, Fort Lauderdale, FL.

Fried, J. and Heinemeier Hanson, D. 2010. *Rework*. Currency, New York.

Fritz, R. 1999. *The Path of Least Resistance for Managers: Designing Organizations to Succeed*. Berrett-Koehler Publishers, Oakland, CA.

Goodwin, D. K. 1998. *Wait Till Next Year: A Memoir*. Simon & Schuster, New York.

Hammer, M. 1997. *Beyond Reengineering: How the Process Centered Organization Is Changing Our Work and Our Lives*. Harper Business, New York.

"Is 16 Too Young to Drive a Car?" *USA Today*, March 2, 2005.

Kendrick, T. 2009. *Identifying and Managing Project Risk: Essential Tools for Failure-Proofing Your Projects*. AMACOM, New York.

Kendrick, T. 2013. *The Project Management Tool Kit*. AMACOM.

Kim, D. 1999. *Introduction to Systems Thinking*. Pegasus Communications, Westford, MA.

Kim, D. 1999. *The Systems Thinking Newsletter*. Pegasus Press, Westford, MA. www.thesystemsthinker.com.

Koenig, M. E. D. "What Is KM? Knowledge Management Explained," *KM World*, May 4, 2012.

Lafley, A. G. and Charan, R. 2008. *Game Changer: How You Can Drive Revenue and Profit Growth with Innovation*. Crown Business, New York.

Leinwand, P. and Mainardi, C. 2016. *Strategy That Works: How Winning Companies Close the Strategy-to-Execution Gap*. Harvard Business Review Press, Cambridge, MA.

Li, C. 2010. *Open Leadership: How Social Technology Can Transform the Way You Lead*. Jossey-Bass, San Francisco, CA.

Maltzman, R. and Shirley, D. 2011. *Green Project Management*. CRC Press, New York.

Martin, R. 2007. *The Opposable Mind: How Successful Leaders Win through Integrative Thinking*. Harvard Business Review Press, Cambridge, MA.

Milton, N. 2009. "Project Lessons Learned Survey." www.nickmilton.com.

Numerous Authors. 1999. *The Capability Maturity Model: Guidelines for Improving the Software Process*. Software Engineering Institute (SEI), Carnegie Mellon University, Reading, MA.

Olson, L. 2017. Last Hope Island: Britain, Occupied Europe, and the Brotherhood that Turned the Tide of War. Random House. New York, New York.

Perry, M. P. 2009. *Business Driven PMO Setup*. J. Ross Publishing, Fort Lauderdale, CA.

Sachs, J. 2015. *The Age of Sustainable Development*. Columbia University Press, New York.

Sawalha, I. H. S. 2013. "Organizational Performance and Business Continuity Management: A Theoretical Perspective and a Case Study." *Journal of Business Continuity and Emergency Planning*, 6(4), 363 (citing British Standards Institution).

Sawalha, I. H. S. and Anchor, J. R. 2012. "Business Continuity Management in Emerging Markets: The Case of Jordan." *Journal of Business Continuity and Emergency Planning*, 5(4), 327–337.

Senge, P. 2005. *The Fifth Discipline*. Doubleday, New York.

Sterman, J. 2000. *Business Dynamics: System Thinking and Modeling for a Complex World*. Irwin McGraw-Hill, New York.

Tice, L. 1997. *Personal Coaching for Results: How to Mentor and Inspire Others to Amazing Growth*. Thomas Nelson Publishers, New York.

Tucker, C. 2008. "Fusing Risk Management and Knowledge Management." *Insight/ASK Magazine*. https://appel.nasa.gov/2008/03/01/fusing-risk-management-and-knowledge-management/.

Wanner, R. 2013. *Project Risk Management: The Most Important Methods and Tools for Successful Projects*. Proconis, Lexington, KY.

Wilkinson, S. 1999. "The Team Friendly Organization Structure: A Paradigm Shift." *PM Network*.

Zahran, S. 1998. *Software Process Improvement: Practical Guidelines for Business Success*. Addison-Wesley, New York.

Author Index

Subject Index

Page numbers followed by *f* indicate figures; those followed by *t* indicate tables.

Underinvestment system archetype,
157–158
Upside risk, 96

V

Vendor management, 13, 131
Vendor risk, 178
Vision, 121, 123*t*, 162

W

Wait Till Next Year (book), xxi
Wal-Mart, 23–24, 103, 158
Watching (Levels of Engagement),
xxiii, 29
WATSON, 103
Well-defined process, 5, 5*f*
Win–win solutions, 142

Printed in the United States
by Baker & Taylor Publisher Services